THE SHORT STORY

THE
SHORT STORY

by
SEAN O'FAOLAIN

MERCIER PRESS

Mercier Press
www.mercierpress.ie

Copyright © by Sean O'Faolain 1948, 1972

First published in the United Kingdom by Collins
in 1948 and in the United States of America
by the Devin-Adair Company.

This edition: Reset 1972,
Reprinted 1983,
Reset and reprinted 2025 by Mercier Press

ISBN: 9781917453233
eISBN: 9781781179901

ACKNOWLEDGEMENTS

The author and publisher are obliged to the following for permission to quote from the stories named: Miss Elizabeth Bowen, Messrs Jonathan Cape Limited, and Alfred A. Knopf Inc: 'Her Table Spread'; the Estate of the late Ernest Hemingway, Messrs Jonathan Cape Limited, and Charles Scribner's Sons: 'The Light of the World'; the Executors of Henry James: 'The Real Thing'; the Estate of the late Frank O'Connor, Messrs Macmillan and Company, and the Macmillan Company: 'In the Train'; Madame Andree Skeffington and the Estate of the late S. S. Koteliansky: for their translations of stories by Daudet, Maupassant, and Chekov.

One is not at all free to write this or that. One does not choose one's subject. That is what the public and the critics do not understand. The secret of masterpieces lies in the concordance between the subject and the temperament of the author.

FLAUBERT *Letters*

CONTENTS

INTRODUCTORY

THE PERSONAL STRUGGLE

THE TECHNICAL STRUGGLE

INTRODUCTORY

1

ON KEEPING THE LINES CLEAR

Many years ago I had the valuable experience of con-
ducting a class in 'The Art of Writing' at one of those
Evening Institutes which the London County Council
maintains in every metropolitan district. I found that,
out of a very large class, only one young woman had any
literary gift; she later published two novels, she would
have done so in any case, and she admitted that she
had really come to my class to pass the time. If I had
published more books at that date, if I had achieved
some reputation, and had time to spare, I might have
been at least of as much encouragement to her as any
writer's interest is to another. As it was I can only hope
that she was sufficiently entertained. I doubt if she got
anything else from the course. Of the rest of the class,
some wished to improve what they charitably called
their English; others wished for a tabloid education
in journalism; others possibly liked to hear somebody
talking in general about books; only two or three really
wished to write. It was for these, in theory the core and
justification of the class, that I could do least of all. I
soon found out that what they really needed was not
instruction in the art of writing but in the art of living.
Intellectually speaking they were not yet adult.

I remember vividly the story one of them showed me
which made me realize how hopeless it is to speak of

technique to an unwakened intelligence. The young man's story opened in his hero's library. It was midnight; as it always is. The firelight flickered on the books; as it always does. The lights were dim; as they always are. The books were bound in calf; the lights of London twinkled outside; there was a decanter and an aroma of cigars . . . I remembered gazing in astonishment at this young man. It was not merely that he knew nothing about this kind of life if it ever quite existed, for he actually lived in a single room on the Cromwell Road, and the smells with which *he* was familiar were petrol and paraffin from the mews. My difficulty was not merely that I could point this out to him—as I did—and beg him to tell me about what he knew. For when I did, and spoke of Coppard and O'Flaherty he cried in dismay:

> But I work in a bank! I go there every morning at nine and leave it at five, and return to my lodgings and, perhaps, go to a cinema, or play squash, and so to bed. It's all very well to talk to me about Coppard. He lives in Hertfordshire or some such place. He is continually meeting quaint characters, villagers and game-keepers, or in and out of the Blue Boar where they tell tall stories. And O'Flaherty has knocked about the world. What experience have I to tell?

This question silenced me utterly. How could I explain to the poor youth that his trouble was not that for him experience did not exist (which is nonsense) but that he himself did not exist? That since he had no perception of his own he had no existence of his own?

There was no use in my telling him that Dickens went to the blacking factory much earlier than nine in the morning and returned much later than five; that Trollope worked in the Post Office for the greater part of his life; or that T. S. Eliot had also worked in a bank; that Maupassant worked as checking-clerk in a government warehouse from 8 a.m. to 6 p.m., at thirty shillings a week, and in four years never had one holiday; that Daudet had been an usher in a school—or that Villon never worked at all. The young man would have gone home and read Daudet and hashed me up a Bouillabaisse Arlésienne; or come back with a story opening outside an old inn-door, with snow falling, and the coach rattling away with horns blowing, and a small boy, and a fat man and only Dickens knows what other borrowed plumes. It was impossible to say anything helpful to him about the technique of writing until his personality came alive.

But would it ever do so? I believed, rather, that I had, standing modestly and eagerly before me, one or other—I could not foretell which—of two of the most extraordinary and inexplicable phenomena of the profession of literature. He was either one of that great host of would-be writers who never get published (except at their own expense) but who never cease to believe that they ought to be published; or he was of that other enormous host who do get published, and who often make money, and whose books are utterly without merit except as gob-stoppers for the perpetual adolescent. Every publisher in the world is familiar with the manuscripts of the former. Every reviewer in the world is familiar with the books of the latter; he either refuses to review them, or gives them a few weary words, or amuses himself at their expense. The libraries are packed with them; people even read them; often, to one's astonishment, the authors achieve some sort of reputation on these books which end in the second-hand barrows, flank to flank with their blood-brothers from the nineteenth century, yellow-backs by authors now quite unknown. Even there, so vendors of second-hand books tell me, they are bought; for if displayed long enough every ragged book will finds its ragged billet. Nothing, it seems, can obliterate the worthless writer short of a world-war. And more go on appearing every week of the year from some of our best publishers. Since their author's names will not figure even in the most learned bibliographies of the future, as their predecessors do not appear in the bibliographies of our time, it is and always will be impossible to give examples One such writer occurs to me from the nineteenth century, and he is not quite unknown (though unread, as Mrs Radcliffe is not unknown, though unread)—George W. M. Reynolds, a man quite famous in his day.

2

Why do these barren trees so eagerly want to bloom? To make money? Not at all. On the contrary, my young man—like these irrepressible middle-brow 'novelists'—was cursed with the highest ideals. If his idea had been to entertain—and be well paid for it— all would be splendid. Indeed if every writer bore in mind more often that it is a large part of his business to entertain—I don't say the main part—how much better all writing would become! Has anything else been more murderous to vitality in fiction than the solemnity that took hold of story-tellers from the time of that assassin Zola onward? But it is more important to ask why these people fail to write. There they are of real interest because their exaggeration of impercipience and insensibility magnifies as on a screen a malady that threatens every writer. There is no writer who has not, at some time, suffered from these same air-blocks in the mental ducts of the pseudo-writer which as effectively stop the personality from functioning as an air-block in a petrol-pipe stops a motor-car. There is no writer who is not horribly familiar with this sensation of seeing his talent cease to flow. 'I'm finished,' he wails. 'I'm written out. I'll never write again.' And then, something happens, and the man is writing as freely as ever. (I note, for instance, that Shaw told Lady Gregory in 1923 that his imagination had vanished, that he was 'done.'[1])

The obstacles to the free flow of talent are often interpreted solely as external enemies, such as neglect, misunderstanding, contumely, domestic circumstances, local conditions. These enemies do exist; few writers have not known them. Yet, the truth is that there are only two 'enemies of promise' that are entirely external and objective, illness and poverty; and I am in doubt even about the poverty. The writer must know, at the start of his career, that he must not only expect all the others but must take them into himself; that they are part of himself, being part of the game; that a book is a writer's circumference, and

[1] *Lady Gregory's Journals.* (Macmillian, 947, p. 213.)

17

that he can only reach his circumference through the radius of his experience. He must know that it will be his care to come to terms with his experience, at the centre; that it will be his chief hope to establish and maintain an equilibrium between his temperament and these, his milieu—an equilibrium that can only be otherwise described as his literary personality. His personality as a man is of no interest to anybody except the people who have to live with him, unless, as does not often happen, it is identical with his personality as a writer.

This, surely, is why some of the finest and most attractive writers have been such objectionable men, quite as scoundrelly as politicians and business-men. Like those, they have aims in view, and obstacles to surmount, and time and again some of the best writers in the world have surmounted them shamelessly and shamefully, by deceit, drink, drugs, hypocrisy, thievery, and even violence. Villon or Corvo or Burns. They are fighting for their own brand of success. They know that everything depends on this equilibrium that they create between temperament and circumstances; that if they fail it will be pointless to say, and indeed dishonest to say, 'Circumstances were too much for me'; that what must be said, rather, is, 'I was not able to cope with my circumstances.' What writer, for example, has not said, and has not felt ashamed immediately he has said it—'If only somebody would give me a private income!'—knowing that to say so is to run away from the battle whose end is always either a good or a bad piece of writing wrested from the tensions of his life.

18

This is the burthen of the whole matter: there can be no evasion for the writer. The man of affairs (like the scientist) can select, and constantly does select what elements in life he will work with; the Argentine, silk-stockings; Murphy, fuel-oil and a limited company, or Devonshire, fertilisers, Sullivan, steam, and private ownership. The writer must accept all the elements, absorb them, transmute them. Baudelaire said this for us, with terrifying persuasiveness, in two sentences in *Les Paradis Artificiels* :

> En effet il est défendu à l'homme sous peine de déchéance et de mort intellectuelle de déranger les conditions primordielles de son existence et de rompre l'équilibre de ses facultés avec les millieux où elles sont destinées a se mouvoir, de déranger son destin pour y substituer une fatalité d'un genre nouveau. Tout homme qui n'accepte pas les conditions de la vie vend son âme.

3

It is in this interior world that we seek the first interest and mystery of the craft of writing. It is here that every artist will try to be most clever and cunning. It is here that he makes his greatest gambles and makes his greatest mistakes. How often has one not heard men plot the recipe for wise self-management. A writer will say, 'I am interested in social questions. This is my real forte. I will concentrate on that.' And if he were Charles Reade he would write his dullest novels about social questions, and his best novels about

Erasmus' father, or Peg Woffington, or a fisher-lass called Christie Johnstone. Antoine François Prévost d'Exiles decided to be a cleric; changed his plan and became a soldier; changed again and became a cleric; decided to write; wrote histories, memoirs, travel-journals, and casually dashed off a little book that made him famous, *Manon Lescaut.* When Daudet received a rebuff with a Provençal play he swore that he would make Fame his handslave; he sat down and spent the rest of his life writing novels which brought him honour and wealth and seemed to guarantee him immortality: he is largely famous because of those little innocent stories about Provence that he wrote in his youth. It was almost by accident that Manzoni, a poet and journalist, wrote what is still, perhaps, the greatest Italian novel. The Goncourts laboured over novel after novel: today nobody reads anything but their diaries, by which they will live for ever. One may easily imagine, since it happened, that a cultivated gentleman of means might say, 'I am interested in the classics. I will write a Platonic dialogue, then I'll translate Aeschylus. Then I might translate Calderon? Yes, this will be my task.' He does all these things, and then he translates an obscure Persian poem—to which nobody pays any great attention when it appears—and is, for ever, famous as the author of *The Rubáiyát of Omar Khayyám.* It was by chance that Cowper wrote *The Task. Robinson Crusoe* was a potboiler. Tennyson toiled at his epics and many now believe that he lives by his lyrics. Tom Moore is remembered not by *Lalla Rookh*, so widely read in the drawing-rooms of his day, but by the *Melodies* sung by ragged Irish emigrants. Flaubert was devoted to *Bouvard et Pecuchet*; nobody else is. Goldsmith wrote but one novel and it is immortal. Of all that John Gay wrote and wrote well, could he ever have counted most for fame on his dramatic piece *The Beggar's Opera?* The examples are endless. Success would seem to be a matter of chance, or of random happy concordance between the man and the subject and the moment, if also one did not recall on the one hand successful deliberate lifelong vocations—Boswell, for example, or Proust, or James Joyce, or Goethe, or Milton or Gibbon—and, on the other hand, perceive obvious reasons for success in *The Vicar of Wakefield* (childhood memories). *Moore's Melodies* (natural patriotic feeling), *Les Lettres de Mon Moulin* (an ideal subject for the warm-hearted Provençal), *The Goncourt Journals* (the perfect work for the temperament of those two wonderful gossips).

It is not, in short, enough to say that if there is genius it will emerge. Genius is a fountain that does not always flow and it mostly wastes itself. 'Full many a flower . . .' It is not enough to say that there is no recipe for success. There is not, but there are dangers to be avoided, temptations to be overcome, obstacles to be manoeuvred, opportunities to be seized. The great thing, I repeat, is not to treat the obstacles as external enemies merely—the stupidity of readers, the contumely of the public, embarrassing local circumstances, which are the stuff of every writer's struggle and which every biographer will record. For the percipient biographer knows that what is really important is what the writer does, within himself, with these obstacles. Indeed, the biographer will (if he is lucky enough to be able to define such occasions) be far less interested in a big material obstacle, such as poverty, than in what seems to be no obstacle at all, such as the influence of a rich wife. He probes for the *hidden* occasions of success or failure; for the vanity, obstinacy, intelligence or resilience of a writer *vis-à-vis* himself; or for the kink that makes the air-block whose result is, perhaps, years of bad writing; or even final silence.

How trivial technique is by comparison with this art! Did Rimbaud become silent because his technical skill failed him? Did Hardy suddenly become less skilled when he wrote *Two on a Tower*? Had Balzac lost his craft when he wrote *Envers de l'Histoire Contemporaine*? Why are so many of Maupassant's stories dismally dull and poor stuff? Admirers of the later Joyce will say that he went from skill to skill, and perhaps he did, but did nothing happen inwardly? I have chosen to write of Daudet because he is one of the saddest examples of the collapse not of skill but of personality; of Chekov because he is one of the most heartening examples of skilful self-management, of the art of keeping the lines clear from beginning to end of the journey. Or, perhaps, it would be a better image to speak of the gardener's art, with hoe and secateurs, that lets in the universe; for when one sees that even the most neglected shrub will flower here and there one must think, 'What a pity that somebody did not give it more attention.'

Nor am I thinking here, solely of the very best writers. To me, at least, it is a pleasure to meet with any writer, even though he may not be a very good writer, the sap of whose personality seems to flow like an unchecked stream. (I say 'seems' for, of course, nobody's does, and one speaks only of their published works, not of the hours and the manuscripts in which it was dammed or failed.) I do not myself count W. W. Jacobs a very good writer, but the apparent ease of his personality gives me great joy. The extent and depth of our satisfaction in all such cases is, of course, limited by the complexity and purity of the personality before us, and chastened by the knowledge that some of the loveliest work has come from the most tormented souls: though even this torment means struggle and effort, like a stream thrusting around boulders. Thus, a modern writer of short-stories whose inner spontaneity never seems to flag is William Saroyan. But our pleasure in this gushing fountain fluctuates according as we perceive, fearfully, some unattractive contamination draining into the fountain from the surrounding American marshes; and we may often have wondered whether the fountain would ever clean itself again. Indeed, this flow of personality is most like a fountain in its tremulous balance and its constant dependence on the source. Mauriac's 'Il faut purifier la source' is only half the truth. The necessary skill is more various than that. There is a lot of plumbing to be done, from time to time, between the source and the jet.

4

No Irish writer, living in a country where circumstances are particularly complicated and difficult for every type of artist—complicated by religion, politics, peasant unsophistication, lack of stimulus, lack of variety, pervasive poverty, censorship, social compression, and so on—can fail to make this observation, or to see the force of it once it is pointed out to him. All about him he can see talent fail or flourish because men are lucky or unlucky—or is it skilful or unskilful?—in this art of self-management. Which may be why Irish writers are far less interested in the technique of writing than in the conditions of writing, though inclined to think exclusively in terms of their own local conditions and to imagine them unique. It is the one theory about which they are as consciously and deeply concerned as French writers are about all sorts of intellectual ideas, including this one. Besides, Irish literature in our time came to its great period of efflorescence in a romantic mood whose concept of a writer was almost like the concept of a priest: you did not just write, you lived writing; it was a vocation; it was a part of the national resurgence to be a writer. A great deal of this was sheer romantic nonsense. There was more talk than work. Yet this art of establishing the conditions, or of avoiding temptations, had to be faced. It was a real, a practical problem. Yeats, for example, knew this art thoroughly: he was always on guard against allurements into which, as any observant biographer will record, he constantly fell, and from which he constantly dragged himself again. Joyce studied himself and the conditions deliberately and with theory. George Moore was translucently clear about what he could and could not get out of Ireland. Æ endlessly discussed the internal combustion engine of the artist.

The names remind us that on this subject there will always be two opposing theories. Æ represents the happy optimist who believes that the so-called 'enemies of promise' are God-sent manna and that the writer need do nothing about it since he is provided by Providence with a spiritual stomach fit to digest even the hardest nails. For example:

> I believe every great writer gets the environment which is right for him, and what the creative poet wants is not other creators about him, but men and women who, either by sympathy or by antagonism, help to evoke his genius. Some kindle by opposition, some by poverty, some by unhappiness as others by comfort and love. Carlyle laid up in brooding on his lonely farm in Scotland the wealth of passionate thought he spent so lavishly on literature, but who but God would have sent his soul to that misery for spiritual food? I feel sure Keats' circumstance, antagonistic or sympathetic, was best for him and he did in fact in that circumstance write more beautiful poetry in his twenty-four years than any other of the English poets in their youth.

I may say that I do not believe one word of this, unless it is implicit that the writer forcefully tames these enemies to serve him; as Æ explicitly says further on when writing on the power of genius to transform its own circumstances:

> Genius has a way of transfiguring those about it by its presence just as a woman in love with a man will reveal to him wit, tenderness and charm she can show to no other. The lover is the master who can evoke melodies others cannot evoke. I have no doubt that in Keats's society his friends were stimulated by his ardent imagination to be brilliant to him in a way they could never seem brilliant to us . . .

But he relapses quickly into his optimistic faith:

> I feel the inevitability of Keats's genius. It evolved
> from within outward by a law of its own being as a
> flower does—taking, indeed, from the sun, the wind,
> the rain, the earth, but, all the time, transmuting
> what it takes inexorably to be of its own nature, to be
> rose and not another flower. I doubt if Keats would
> have been different in quality or character, though
> the choice of subject might have been different, if
> he had never met Hunt or others of his circle. He
> moved to his own perfection as irresistibly as the
> acorn moves to be oak and not another tree.

Many of us who heard Æ say such things had to handle much more difficult material, and in much more exacting times, than he, and we were not greatly comforted by this optimism. But he had plenty else to say that Irishmen interpreted accurately in terms of their local conditions. This on the chauvinists, for example, was a clear-headed advice to us all to avoid the temptation of patriotism:

> The idea that literature can be shaped from outside
> in response to the popular demand dies hard. When a
> genius is found he absolutely refuses to do any of the
> things the sentimentalists expects of him. He is just as
> likely to kick his country as to bless it. He follows a law
> of his own being which means that he can only express
> what is in him and not in the minds of other people.

And this is wise: 'I think a poet ought to be shy about his public if not altogether unconscious of it.'

26

Or:

> If you think of fame, large circulations, income, you must be deflected from disinterestedness. What you do is no longer an exquisite soliloquy between yourself and heaven.

Or this, against the danger of 'general ideas', such as religious ideas:

> The slightest personal experience of the spirit is worth *as poetry* more than all the greatest ideas of the world's greatest teachers, repeated with no matter how much reverence.

Or, one of his favourite and often-repeated aphorisms: 'The important thing about a poet is finally this: "Out of how deep a life does he speak." '[1]

Yeats, on the other hand, believed in a deliberately concocted personality. Indeed he developed, finally, an elaborate theory of Self and Antiself which, I think, was no more than the device of a gregarious man to avoid the pitfalls of his own natural gregariousness on the one hand, and to compensate and comfort, himself, on the other, for a constitutional inability to achieve successfully with that gregarious Self in the common gregarious world, the world of action in which he constantly craved to 'cut a dash.' Thus:

> To oppose the new ill-breeding of Ireland, which may in a few years destroy all that has given Ireland

---

[1] I take these quotations from *The Living Torch*, edited by Monk Gibbon. (Macmillan, 1937.)

a distinguished name in the world . . . I can only set up a secondary or interior personality created out of the tradition of myself, and this personality (alas only possible to me in my writings) must be always gracious and simple. It must have that slight separation from interests which makes charm possible, while remaining near enough for passion.

One could give dozens of examples of this; all implying that literature is not merely an external technique, or something that works of itself, but is dependent of a careful inward control of personality for a literary end. This truth is embedded in the excess, and even in the nonsequiturs, of many of his pontifications, such as this:

> As life goes on we discover that certain thoughts sustain us in defeat, or give us victory, whether over ourselves or others; and it is these thoughts, tested by passion, that we call convictions. Among subjective men (that is in all those who must spin a web out of their own bowels) the victory is an intellectual daily recreation of all that exterior fate snatches away . . .

Which is but another way of saying that the literary personality is what we win from life for literature.

To this danger, and the remedy of inward withdrawal, he comes again and again; in the aphorism that 'We make out of the quarrel with others rhetoric, out of the quarrel with ourselves poetry'; or in the warning, that:

> Argument, the moment victory is sought, becomes a clash of interests. One should not—above all in books, which sigh for immortality—argue at all if not

ready to leave to another apparent victory. In daily life one becomes rude the moment one grudges to the clown his perpetual triumph.

5

George Moore is one of the most interesting examples of the losses and the gains of the subjective plumber. Joseph Hone, in his biography of Moore, has an acute passage on Moore's technique in *Hail and Farewell*: It describes his method—in this book, his masterpiece, for it was wholly and magnificently successful,—of deliberately coining a suitable literary personality for (and out of) the stresses of the occasion:

> For the purposes of his book his business was to cultivate an ironical and detached personality, constructing a complex humour out of an appearance of paradoxical simplicity, and to see himself, even in the matter of his anti-Catholic passion, as others saw him, while remaining the hero of his book.

This is exactly the sort of position, or vantage point, that Moore kept seeking all his life; changing it from period to period; even from book to book; so successfully that no biographer can ever hope to define the man, since he was, in effect, not merely a work of art but many works of art. But he himself makes no secret of this fact that he passed from phase to phase, and, indeed, I think he becomes less amusing and less interesting, if not actually uninteresting, in the latter part of his life when he rests at one vantage point, that of the accomplished and impersonal stylist to whom a Greek tale (*Daphnis and Chloe*), an Irish tale (*A Story-teller's Holiday*), or a Biblical tale (*The Brook Kerith*) comes with equal ease and without special mental adjustments or any apparent special convictions.

The influences to which Moore submitted himself were, for the most part, literary, though there were also friends, such as that Hawkins who is the 'Marshall' of *Confessions of a Young Man*, or John Oliver Hobbes (Mrs Craigie) who, in his biographer's words, 'furbished him up,' or Lady Cunard; and his admiration for Degas and Manet must have encouraged him in his early naturalistic phase. Such bookish influences, a commonplace in every writer's development, have a special interest in Moore's case because of his suggestive vocabulary when describing them, and because he noted them, sifted them, accepted them and rejected them, when their work was done, with an unusually ruthless circumspection.

Zola's influence, for example, carried him through *A Modern Lover, A Mummer's Wife* and *A Drama in Muslin*, but not much farther. 'I owe you everything,' he says to Zola, after publishing the first; and while writing *A Mummer's Wife* he said, 'I have hopes of being Zola's offspring in England.' But while he is at *A Drama in Muslin* it appears that he has already begun to realize the deficiencies of Zola's instrument for rendering the more poetical aspects of life, although he still follows the 'master'. Two years later, however, in appreciating Turgenev in the *Fortnightly Review*, he makes it clear that he now realizes that the naturalistic technique of objective reproduction (I quote Hone) 'is a dream and not even a beautiful dream: Flaubert's so-called impersonality is the vainest of delusions, and Turgenev, even in his narration of physical phenomena, gives utterance to a thought and manifests his own spirit.' Zola is thereupon not only cast aside, but overthrown with taunts and mockery that pursue the fallen idol to the end of his days. Not that Zola was troubled. 'It is the law of nature,' he said. 'Dans la littérature il faut toujours tuer son père.'

The same fate overtook Ireland, which gave Moore his best book *Hail and Farewell*, and, the turning point in his literary career, *The Lake*. Once he had sucked it dry he spat it out for ever. The same is true of his treatment of all his guides, save only Balzac. For what he says of one of his friends applies also to books—making all allowance for his usual bravado and his love of semi-comic exaggeration:

> I used him [he says] without shame or stint, as I have used all those with whom I have been brought in close contact. I cannot recall a case of man or woman who ever occupied any considerable part of my thoughts that did not contribute towards my moral or physical welfare. In other words, and in col-loquial language, I never had useless friends hanging about me.

Or, again: 'Never could I interest myself in a book if it were not the exact diet my mind required at the time, or in the very immediate future.'

He has a curious phrase about books—he uses it more than once and it recalls Flaubert's phrase about choosing subjects in concordance with one's

31

temperament: they 'awaken the voice of conscience.' He goes on:

> Books are like individuals; you know at once whether they are going to create a sense within the sense, to fever, to madden you in blood and brain, or if they will merely leave you indifferent . . . Many are the reasons for love but I confess I only love woman or book when it is a voice of conscience, never heard before, heard suddenly, a voice I am at once endearingly intimate with.

Elsewhere he speaks of a writer being 'out of tune with the spring of my aspirations'; in another place of Gautier introducing him to 'the plain simple conscience of the pagan world'; elsewhere, he refers to 'Affinities in literature corresponding to, and very analogous to sexual affinities'; and when, finally, he comes to Balzac, he hails him as 'the great moral influence of my life.' This vocabulary, clearly, has not a merely technical reference: it is the vocabulary of expanding personality, the more impressive in that it comes from a writer whose preoccupation with form and style is the first thing that his name suggests.

Moore is fair game for both the optimists and the pessimists, for those who believe that God does our spiritual plumbing for us and those who believe that we have to do it ourselves. For it can be said that the result of these equilibria that Moore thus established between his temperament and his milieu has not been, all told, a very interesting personality, or series of personalities. (One must not, in this, judge him by a few books; and one must consider whether his entire *œuvre* has a recognizable unity. There are eighty-three items in the short bibliography appended to Hone's *Life*.) I would, myself, agree that the only indisputable success is the masterly concoction in *Hail and Farewell*, and that all his other personalities have a distinct air of contrivance and unpersuasiveness. But if the optimists were to say, with a mixture of impatience and good nature, 'Why did he not write out of his own simple, natural self?' what one has to reply is that the 'simple, natural self' of George Moore was that of an ignorant oaf, very vain, cunning it is true, fond of horses, who could not spell, knew no grammar, had received no education, had, it is also true, an evident gift—for he dragged it out and put it to work like a slave-driver—but who, had he remained in Ireland and run true to type, would have been a typical country squireen, High Sheriff of Mayo and the possible breeder of Grand National winners like his grandfather. 'But he didn't, you see!' cry the Divine Plumbers. 'So there is no more to be said.' Surely, if there ever was a writer whose painful efforts to manage his own nature and circumstances make nonsense of this Divine Plumber theory, it is George Moore.

6

'The simple, natural self!' I wonder whether it has ever existed in any creative writer? I think it may briefly exist, though in what purity nobody can say, at the start of a writer's career. But very soon everything help to make him self-conscious. His friends' comments on what he writes affect him even before he publishes at all; his struggles to take each new redoubt of experience;

the critics' remarks when he does publish; a growing critical sense in himself, about life, culminating in the point where he begins to consider in his writing the implications of his experience as a man—a condition of mind induced hourly by love, lust, sorrow, death, illness, poverty, manifested in a thousand different incidents, every one of them a question-mark. There are writers whose 'simple, natural self' carries them a long way; to their thirties even. It is ultimately and inevitably overlaid, or it betrays the man. That period when a man is approaching forty is the dreadful test period for all artists. If they have prepared for it; if they have developed, if they have won resilience they will move into a new phase, and perhaps then go on to the end still creative. Otherwise they repeat themselves, mechanically, or stop.

There is something very affecting about a young writer's first book. One sees the youth fondling the petals of life, with the happy wonder of youth, or grasping life with the passion and pride of youth's self-confidence and naked strength. The readers of such books (one is presuming a book of some evident quality) always tend to over-praise them, so warm are our feelings at this spectacle, so full of affectionate apprehension for the future. And the young man or woman, full of confidence, accepts such praise as no more than due! What the critic rarely says, for it is pointless to say it at this stage, is that the very source of the charm of such books is also their weakness—that untutored wonder, that fearless eagerness, so breathless that it obviously does not in the least know what it is about. 'Ah, yes,' the older critic says to himself, 'you have life in your hands. It *is* lovely, it *is* dreadful, it *is* wonderful, isn't it?

That you should feel this and convey that you feel this is why we praise you so much. You have the rude stuff of literature in you. Now, in your next book, and your next book after that, we shall see what you have to say about it all. Your stories have a natural vagueness and inconclusiveness now—your wonder and eagerness are the natural cause of that. The next time you will clarify with the personal, the original, the different-to-every-body-else comment? Won't you?' Or as Flaubert wrote to Madame Maupassant about young Guy's first stories: 'As time goes on he will gain in originality. He will get a personal way of seeing and feeling, and that is everything.' And what he adds is as significant, if we interpret it in the same sense of 'personal' as against 'general': 'The chief thing in this world is to maintain one's soul in a lofty region, far from the bourgeois and democratic mud and mire.'

It is at this stage that the 'simple, natural self' begins to disappear. The simple, natural self is a mere embryo self, a virginal self, as yet unmarried to and un-mauled by experience. But, to be sure, what we mean by experience is undefinable because it is as different for every writer as every writer is different from his neighbour—and grows more and more so as he develops this enlarged and assertively personal way of seeing and feeling. To revert to my young man of the Literary Institute, he thought that experience means adventure. The death of a cat will suffice; a child's tears; a friend-ship ruined; an unkind teacher; a sad day; a holiday in the country; the harebell's touch . . .' One thinks of Jane Austen and there is no more to be said. The adventure is interior. The personality can be developed, or concocted, or created out of apparently nothing at all.

It all depends on the sensitivity of the person, and on his imperviousness to conventional ideas, 'the democratic mud and mire.'

When, therefore, I was asked to write a book on the Craft of the Short Story it seemed evident to me that this is the first lesson that the young writer must, I will not say learn, because it cannot be taught, but expect to endure. He can learn at least that he ought to be ready to endure this. I have grown up in a country where young men and women are daily taught and have obediently imbibed the opposite; namely, that every large problem has been settled long ago and that there is no need to ask any more questions, because our two divinely appointed spiritual plumbers, the Church and Cathleen ni Houlihan, will look after all that *in vitam aeternam, amen.* How can one induce a young writer to see the truth that, on the contrary, the moment an opinion becomes popular he must, as a writer, at once abandon it? The moment an idea becomes general it is useless to the individual artist, except possibly as a general assumption like Balzac's Royalism. To be a Fabian when almost everybody else is a Tory can be of assistance to a writer: to be a Tory when everybody else is a Socialist may at least prevent him from becoming the tool of the mob. It will aways be difficult to make the young writer accept this proposition. Society is a conspiracy on the part of the many to defend the conventionality of the weak and to discredit the originality of the strong. It is constantly pillorying writers whose points of view offend its conventions—Flaubert, Maupassant and Hardy are modern examples. Every writer is subconsciously aware that this is so. One can see this unconscious self-protection at work in English writers today, for no sooner does the public take over their ideas, which have been the stuff of their poetry for years, than they at once sheer away from these ideas and look for others. There was hardly an Irish writer who was not on the side of the movement for Irish political independence; immediately it was achieved they became critical of the nation. It is this that makes all politicians say that writers are an unreliable tribe. They are. It is their *métier*.

7

It may be thought that this approach to the craft of writing is to strike a subjective note alien both to criticism and literature in English. I do not think so. Admittedly not many English writers have been interested in the subjective aspects of criticism; agreed, too, that the English mind tends, of its nature, to the sturdy belief that personal integrity is one of those things that looks after itself, or is attended to at School, and if not then nothing more can be done about it—a pragmatism that has, over large periods, been magnificently justified in literature. But it has not always sufficed, and it is one of the most dangerous delusions of the foreigner (and one of the most dangerous pretensions of Englishmen themselves) that the English nature has not a deeply subjective strain and an unpredictable emotional inflammability. E. M. Forster has an excellent image for the English genius: he compares it to a dolphin, which is seen only when it is not diving. What dark, emotional stresses must have groaned behind the outward vigour of the Elizabethans! From the death of Shakespeare to the death of Dryden poetry was unashamedly subjective and, almost of theory, self-conscious. And who would say that seventeenth century prose was extrovert? The physical pride and conquest of the nineteenth century has overlaid this aspect of the Englishman's nature so effectively that it was not until our own generation that English poets began to realize again those other strains in their composition, and their possibilities, and by harking back to this secretive metaphysical note in the national character—I dare call it a self-lacerating note—helped poetry to recover from the impasse of nineteenth century optimism.

As for prose, English fiction has always been triumphantly extrovert: in this context I would say fatally triumphant. To the death of Dickens it had such a long line of triumphs that there might have seemed no earthly reason to believe that the tradition was not endlessly fertile. Before Elba it was already flourishing with (to mention only four novelists—two Irish and two English) Scott, Jane Austen, Maria Edgeworth, Lever; and then, what names!—Dickens, the Brontes, Thackeray, Trollope, George Eliot, R. L. S., Borrow. . . . But when the great names still went on, to the threshold of our own time, nobody in England sufficiently remarked that it was not the same novel, that Meredith, Henry James, Conrad and Hardy were not in the old extrovert English tradition, but in a subjective Continental tradition. They did not notice because criticism (James apart) was John Bullishly unaware that thanks to France and Russia the Novel had now surpassed the achievement of the Drama; that Shakespeare, for example, is equalled by Balzac; that nobody else in the theatre equals Dostoievsky, Tolstoy or Turgenev for insight into human nature, wit, social interest or even—dare I say the horrid words?—mere 'educative value.' But that the Russian, French and English novel is, therefore, as fit a subject for study in the schools and universities is even not yet fully admitted anywhere outside America.

I suppose no university in Britain thinks the short-story other than a modern toy.

The nineteenth century's reverence for the purely English tradition in literature was fatal to the development of fiction. The French and the Russians were ready for that emotional and intellectual break-up of the nineteenth century which is scarcely reflected in Dickens or Thackeray or George Eliot. The implications of *Madame Bovary*, for example, did not even remotely touch Dickens who was at the date of its publication writing *Little Dorrit*. Life in Britain was too stable. English novelists (with rare exceptions, like that kindly man, Charles Kingsley) were either unaware of or indifferent to the rise of the worker, the decay of the Church, the increase in scepticism, the evil social effects of the industrial revolution, the growing influence of science on education, the crumbling away of the old traditional moral values. Britain was largely protected from all that the Continent was experiencing on its own body: compared to the social history of France from 1815 to 1914 the history of Britain is a blissful blank. This emotional turmoil reflected, indeed documented, in the French and Russian novel and short-story, and in the drama of the northerners, is not to be sought for in the English novel, which retains its extrovert, easy-going, good-natured and generally good-humoured attitude to life and to itself to, and beyond, the turn of the century.

French influence only came into English fiction around the 1880's. It was then a mere trickle. There was nobody to 'boost' it as Brandes, Archer and Shaw 'boosted' Ibsen. In any case the library system was altogether against the realistic type of novel, faithfully reflecting the same sort of public feeling that made Hardy stop writing novels after the rebuffs to *Jude the Obscure* in 1895. Hardy aside, George Gissing must have been one of the first qualified practitioners of the new fiction: then Galsworthy; but was there an earlier popular success than Bennett's *Old Wives' Tale* in 1908? (It predates Wells's *Mr Polly* by two years.) After that naturalism became a flood, an all too obvious flood that still swamps the English novel generations after it has been discredited abroad. Indeed Bennett was an example of a man who 'got' naturalism as another man might 'get' religion, and so little else: so little of the poetic feeling, the subtlety, wit, romantic lyricism, sceptical intelligence, truculence, passion, form and style that accompanied the mode in France and justified it, and, when it had exhausted itself, remained behind like treasures thrown up by the tide.

For this there is an interesting explanation (which also gives us, a useful date) in an essay written as late as 1899 by Virginia Crawford on 'The Present Decadence in France':

There never has been a time when French authors have been so widely studied, so freely translated as at present. Not an editor of a serious magazine but feels that an article on the newest French poet or novelist forms an essential feature of his monthly

equipment. It is as indispensable as soup at a din-
ner-party. Unfortunately for our powers of discern-
ment, not for long years has France been so poor
in great men as at the present moment ... Of this
the British public remains all unconscious, and
the study and admiration which, thirty years ago
we might have bestowed with advantage on Balzac
and Flaubert, on Theophile Gautier and the du
Goncourts, we bestow today in foolish abundance
on Marcel Prévost and Anatole France, on Bourget
and 'Gyp.'

As for the great Russian writers of novels and stories, they only began to trickle into England after
Vizetelly started his publishing house in 1879.[1] (It
was he who introduced Zola's works to the English
public.) The 'Slavs,' as they used to be called, were
admired, but with grave reservations as to their sanity,
that indispensable English virtue more dear to husband and matron than chastity itself, more admired by
writers and critics than anything else except humour,
even more admired than passion or imagination.
That same essay of Virgina Crawford's declares that
Turgenev, for example, is still unknown at that date
(1899) to the mass of British readers: but with some
excuse (although the Constance Garnett translations had begun to appear) since even in Paris he
is 'quite unfamiliar to the rising literary generation'.
With this Henry James's essay on Turgenev (1884),
in *Partial Portraits*, agrees. And I have gone through
eight volumes of *Les Contemporains* by Jules Lemaître

[1]I believe the English put him in jail for it.

41

(c. 1884-1914) without finding a single essay on him, or on any Russian writer; though, for that matter, he does not consider any English book except Stanley's *Through Darkest Africa*. The result of this extraordinarily tardy and impure infiltration of European influence into the novel was that the transition away from the nineteenth century English tradition occurred imperceptibly, and it may yet not be admitted fully: although it would now be impossible for those who might deny it to name a modern novelist of genuine quality in English who writes in the tradition of Scott or Thackeray or George Eliot rather than in the tradition of Balzac and Flaubert and Zola.

This change which, in our time, has come over the novel and poetry in England has not appreciably affected the short-story. If one were to list the first twelve or fifteen most interesting modern writers of short-stories in English that occur to the mind, who would they be? James Joyce, George Moore, Liam O'Flaherty, Elizabeth Bowen, Frank O'Connor, H. E. Bates, A. E. Coppard, V. S. Pritchett, Hemingway, Saroyan, Malamud, William H. Gass, Nabokov, Nadine Gordimer, Jean Stafford . . . The observation that at once forces itself on us is that only three are English. There are, of course, other good American, Irish and English short-story writers: they will not be offended if they have not occurred to me as readily as these. Yet, though another critic would have other preferences, I think the proportion would not much alter. The Americans and the Irish do seem to write better stories. One is tempted to say that the English nature does not take kindly to the short form; that it requires scope; and James, Meredith, Hardy and Conrad seem to support this.[1] But, then, Turgenev's stories are not commonly brief, and I cannot think that it matters greatly if a writer prefers, say, six thousand words to three thousand.

Indeed I think every freedom of method must be granted to a writer, including scope, if he requires it. As Maupassant puts it, in the foreword to *Pierre et Jean*:

> Tous les écrivains, Victor Hugo comme M. Zola, ont réclamé avec persistance le droit absolu, droit indisputable, de composer, c'est-à-dire d'imaginer ou d'observer, suivant leur conception personelle de l'art. Le talent provient de l'originalité, qui est une manière spéciale de penser, de voir, de comprendre et de juger. Or, le critique qui prétend à définir le roman suivant l'idée qu'il s'en fait d'après les romans qu'il aime, et d'établir certaines règles invariables de composition, luttera toujours contre un tempérament d'artiste apportant une manière nouvelle.

It is this essential personal freedom which, I feel, points the weakness of English writers of short-stories. They do not desire to avail themselves of it. The 'tempérament d'artiste apportant une manière nouvelle' does not ride them. The fact is that the Enlish

---

[1] The little story is but scantily relished in England, where readers take their fiction rather by the volume than by the page, and the novelist's idea is apt to resemble one of those old-fashioned carriages which require a wide court to turn round. In America. . . the short tale has had a better fortune.' Henry James, *Partial Portraits*, p. 264.

do not admire the artistic temperament: they certainly do not demonstrate it; nor do they cultivate avidly the 'manière spéciale de penser, de voir, de comprendre et de juger.' Yet, surely, the obvious distinctive element in the short-story—distinguishing it from every other art—is its shortness: i.e., the fact that the writer has deliberately selected some special incident or character; and that there can, or should be, only one reason for this—because it is (to quote Maupassant again) 'in good concordance with all the tendencies of his thought. 'In other words the short story is an emphatically personal exposition. What one searches for and what one enjoys in a short story is a special distillation of personality, a unique sensibility which has recognized and selected at once a subject that, above all other subjects, is of value to the writer's temperament and to his alone—his counterpart, his perfect opportunity to project himself. The reader acknowledges this to be so when he speaks of a 'good Hemingway,' or 'a good Coppard'; or when he says—'That story is pure Chekov,' or admits ownership in a distinctive point of view by saying, 'That is a Maupassant situation.'

Why America should produce interesting personalities in the short-story I simply do not understand unless it be that American society is still unconventionalized. The fact is that it does produce them. It is plain enough why Ireland does, an unconventional and still comparatively human people, in spite of our latter-day doctrinaire chauvinism. France, clearly, is, as she has always been, the breeding ground of the personal and original way of looking at things, expounded with intelligence and defended with disruptive. passions, a virtue

44

as fruitful in art as it is fatal in politics. It is the primary thing in the short-story which is, of its nature, a pointing finger.

One does not wish to pursue too far this subject of English diffidence about seeing things in an assertively personal way; any subject pursued too hard will turn on the hunter and eat him. I push it a little farther only because the point has to be made, sooner or later, by everybody who deals with the short-story; because, in turn, Maupassant insists on bringing it up, both in practice and theory. See the Preface to *Pierre et Jean* from which I have already quoted. It forced itself on Henry James when he wrote, so brilliantly, about Maupassant, extracting from him the shrewd remark that whereas the writer in the English tradition will always have the courage of his opinions ('when it befalls that we have opinions') it is the way of the French to have the courage of their perceptions. By this he means that the French say what they see—with the proper reservation that they tend to see so brutally, and, even, perhaps too often, to the exclusion of all indulgence, kindness or reticence; whereas it is in the English tradition to nourish the fruits of good-humour and piety, in the civil and domestic sense, of the love of sport, the sense of decorum, the habit of respect, the absence of irony, the expansive tendency of the race, the emphasis on pragmatic action, all of which mitigate the Englishman's emotional tensions, irritations and nervous exasperations; and all of which assuagement, one may add, the French will end up by calling Anglo-Saxon hypocrisy. In short, the English way of looking at life is much more social and much less personal and individual than the French, and this

way of life, one may well think, does work more effectively inside the broad frame of the novel, which is in
the nature of a sweeping gesture over a large landscape of life, rather than in the short-story, which is,
no matter how lyrical, *ad hoc.* In dealing, later, with
Maupassant and Chekov this may become more clear;
at the moment I merely wish to underline that the
'artistic temperament' of which Maupassant speaks is
essentially a personal temperament bringing to bear
on life, as he insists, a personal way of seeing, and a
personal way of saying.

I am back at my young man of the Literary Institute,
our would-be writer of short-stories, wishful to learn
the craft of writing before he has even begun to think
of the craft of being himself. What better can I do for
such young men than to draw their attention first of
all to the inside story behind the work of three such
masters of the short-story as Daudet, Chekov and
Maupassant—the personal struggle behind the literary
problem. Then we can pass on to the more popular
idea of 'technique.'

THE PERSONAL STRUGGLE

2

ALPHONSE DAUDET
OR *THE INTERRUPTED ROMANTIC*

Daudet was the local boy who made good; *le petit chose* who became *grand chose.* He has been compared, over and over, to Dickens, for this, for remaining this always, for his unspoiled sense of wonder as of perpetual boyhood, for his exuberant love of children, for his frequent autobiographical use of his childhood, for his readiness to be melodramatic about his first sorrows, triumphs and disappointments. He is at his best when he is most touching, most touching when he is remembering, and when he is remembering he is all 'Oh!' and 'Ah!' and 'Quels braves gens!' with such sighing, kindly laughter that one feels that even when he was very young he must have been what in Ireland we call 'crabit', or 'crabbed,' meaning old-head-on-young-shoulders; so that for him to grow old meant little change. Those pages in his memoirs that describe his arrival in Paris, as a lad, one foggy wintry morning, shoving his bag in a truck across the dawn-grey city, waiting about for the *crèmerie to* open, after two days' journey up from the south, without food, then making great castles-in-the-air over the raisins and the nuts with his brother Ernest before he retired to his garret to write poetry for a year—those pages when set side by side with his charming account of his first play, to see which he travelled up again from the south, this time from Morocco, reveal that nor mood nor mind have changed over the passing years.[1] Whether he is fifteen or fifty he is just as ready to feel madly gay at one moment and to weep the next. He was one of those people who are by nature so happy that they enjoy a good cry. It was Daudet's triumph never to grow up. It was also his great weakness to want to write 'grown-up.' That is the burthen of this essay.

If Æ was right in thinking that the gods send us misfortune for our own good then Daudet was lucky in having a father who was as unlucky as Micawber, and whose ruin bestowed on his children the ineffable blessing of an early introduction to the cruelty of life. It may, in that case, have been a misfortune for him that his mother, Adeline Reynaud, came (like Mrs Micawber) from a good family, the best people in Nîmes, a woman of a much more delicate soul than Vincent Daudet, who was a peasant's son. Alphonse's first step towards the scene of his triumphs, Paris, was due to his father's business difficulties: when he was nine they moved from Nîmes to Lyons, along that Rhône which he never forgot and which gave him so many delightful scenes, gave him, indeed, the stuff of immortality. It was in Lyons that his papa's fortunes failed and from there that-Madame Daudet, poor soul, had to return to her own people at Nîmes; and it was from there that the others had to set out into the cold world to earn a living. Daudet's first job was to be usher in a college at Alais. His misery there, compared sometimes with little David Copperfield's, gave us his

[1] *Quarante Ans de Paris.* Genève, 1945.

novel *Le Petit Chose*, or rather the first and better half of it, with himself as the Daniel and his brother Ernest as the Jacques of the story.

He fondled the petals of life early; at fifteen he had written a novel, now lost, and was already known in Lyons as a writer. When he found, at seventeen, that Ernest was able to earn a living in Paris as a journalist he went there to join him, living in cold and hunger, as one may read in his memoirs or in the second and less affecting part of *Le Petit Chose*. In Paris he wrote pieces for *Figaro*, carefully pumicing every line. He wrote verse. At eighteen he published a book of poetry, *Les Amoureuses*, of which the pretty narrative poem 'Les Prunes' is deservedly well-known, both because it is charming in itself and because on the strength of it the Empress Eugénie induced the Duc de Morny to make the youth his secretary. (Blessed days when a book of verse was a recommendation to office.) These personalities remind us that he grew up in the heyday of the Second Empire.

'Les Prunes' has all his natural grace and effortlessness. It is a picture of a little boy and his girl-cousin meeting on his uncle's farm. They enter the orchard. She covets the plums. They gather them together:

> *Elle en prend une, elle la mord.*
> *Et, me l'offrant : 'Tiens !' me dit-elle.*
> *Mon pauvre cœur battait si fort,*
> *Elle en prend une ; elle la mord.*
> *Ses petites dents sur le bord*
> *Avaient fait des points de dentelle . . .*
> *Elle en prend une, elle la mord.*
> *Et, me l'offrant :'Tiens !' me dit-elle.*

Ce fut tout, mais ce fut assez ;
Ce seul fruit disait bien des choses.
(Si j'avais su ce que je sais !)
Ce fut tout, mais ce fut assez.
Je mordis, comme vous pensez,
Sur la trace des lèvres roses :
Ce fut tout, mais ce fut assez ;
Ce seul fruit disait bien des choses . . .

One is tempted to build on two verses a whole criticism and appreciation of Daudet's gifts; his tenderness, the lightness and slightness of his material, his gaiety, his butterfly fancy, and, above all, that impressively happy temperament, that famous 'charm' which defies analysis and of which nobody has ever been able to say anything better than Jules Lemaître, who described it as a wild flower of nature in the cultivated garden of literature.

Plays come next—fatal plays, for they gave him a taste of success and they introduced him to the humiliation of public failure, as we shall see. He collaborated with L'Epine for *La Dernière Idole*, which went on at the Odéon, and, at the age of twenty-five, he saw his *L'Oillet Blanc* at the Théâtre Français. His duties with Morny were slight. He had time to wander about a good deal, to Algiers, to Corsica, to Sardinia. He met fellow Provençals, including Mistral. In 1863 he retired to romantic solitude in the old ruined mill at Fontvieille, in the Rhône Valley, from which he was to send out, from 1866 on, the exquisite and immortal short stories collected in 1869 as *Les Lettres de Mon Moulin*. He was sketching the outlines of *Le Petit Chose*, the first part of which appeared in Paris in 1867, when he was twenty-seven. He had been gathering since 1861 the materials for *Tartarin*, which appeared in 1872. The much later novel *Numa Roumestan* stems from the same region and the same preoccupation with the ways and manner of the south. All his devotion, one observes, is still to Provence. It is his constant joy to recreate it, to tease it, even to mock at it, but always to desire to possess it. That first love seems to us, today, to have given him everything. All the magnificence of the 'Vénus terrestre' of the capital seemed, then, powerless against the dusty plains, the pines and oaks, the hot vineyards, the little towns, the exasperating, lovable people of Languedoc. The Rhône was more enchanting than the Seine. Arles, Nîmes, Beaucaire, Tarascon were the names of his girls. These *Lettres* are love-letters to Provence, as *Numa Roumestan* is the sort of loving, bitter letter a man may write to a woman after it is 'all over'.

How shall one write the love-story of Alphonse Daudet? So natural in its course, so familiar, so fatal. It is one of the favourite themes of French novelists: the gradual domination of Paris. It is, with a difference of temperament and values but not of ambition, the story of Eugène de Rastignac. One cannot help thinking of Daudet when one reads the story of the provincial and tender-minded young man, de Gèry, in *The Nabab*, arrested, shocked, enthralled by the capital. In his memoirs Daudet tells of a pathetic and amusing fellow named Philoxene Boyer who became, he says, the victim of a book; he wished to squander his wealth, to kiss the tips of the fingers of duchesses, to be received in Paris society because he had read *Père Goriot*, and he did squander his patrimony, in six months; then he read *Hamlet* and spent his life amid mountainous piles of books writing, never finishing, *the* definitive comment on Shakespeare. Perhaps Daudet read too many books, also: the tyranny of Zola's documentary method lies heavily on every one of the novels; there are echoes all the while from Balzac—even in such sub-titles as 'Mœurs Parisiennes' or 'Mœurs Conjugales.'

But this young provincial did not take Paris as a mistress, in enslavement to her sensual and superficial excitements and delights. He married a very charming woman, Julia Allard, in 1867, intelligent, of gentle birth like his mother, a sensitive and delicate writer, the daughter of two writers. It was one of the happiest marriages in the history of letters. It was too happy.

It is essential to notice how long Daudet resisted the 'Vénus terrestre.' He came to Paris in 1857. He made no real effort to possess her until 1874: that is the date of his first novel of Parisian manners, *Froment Jeune et Risler Aîné.* He had enjoyed Paris, been astonished and excited by it, but he was for years too palpitatingly southern, too reckless, too febrile, too uncalculating to be more than astonished and excited by this, to him, foreign city. For Paris, I think it is Henry James who first observed it, to its provincials, even to Parisians, seems to retain, always, a quality of being strange and foreign, difficult if not impossible to tame. It is true that French writers preserve a sense of the wonder of their capital that the writers of other countries do not feel about theirs. French writers apostrophize Paris, glorify it, abuse it, over and over again, in every period, like men assaulting a mystery. With the exception of Dickens I know no English writer who conveys anything of this sense of a lust to possess London, like Joyce's lust for Dublin. It came to Daudet only after he settled down in Paris; that is, after—had he only known it, had the critics only known it as they did not—he had already achieved his immortality through his stories of the South. Of this there is no question. What he wrote afterwards did, in the prudent words of Edmund Gosse, place him 'for the moment at all events, near the head of contemporary European literature.' Time has shown that his short stories had placed him there already, and that his later novels, which brought him so much fame and wealth, not only add little to, his reputation but utter a challenge which idolaters of his stories would far prefer not to have to accept.

2

People do not read the books of Julia Allard nowadays. She wrote beautifully. She wrote as nearly all women write, with a delicate precision as to her impressions, a sensitive wariness about her own emotions, very alert, on the watch, sympathetic, miniscule. There is a fascinating essay on her in Jules Lemaître's *Les Contemporains*, hung largely on her *Enfance d'une Parisienne*. He proposes there that the one gift women writers do not develop is the *don pittoresque*, the gift of making pictures. His example is amusing. 'L'oiseau fait entendre sous le feuillage son chant joyeux.' That, he suggests, is how a woman writer will say it. An observation dissolving into a feeling. But Madame de Sévigné very beautifully says, 'C'est joli! Une feuille qui chante.'

Would not a man, however, have omitted the 'C'est joli!'? (Daudet would not. Conrad was put off by him just because he could never cease from gripping one's arm, pointing, crying out in astonishment.)

Here is an example of her style: the Children's Ball as Madame Daudet remembered it, for she, too, is a lover of childhood memories in Paris:

> Déjà dès en entrant on entendait un peu de musique, de petits pieds ébranlant le parquet, et des bouffées de voix confuses. Je prends la main d'une petite Alsacienne en corsage de velours, et maintenant voici l'éblouissement des glaces, des clartés. Le pianc étouffé, assourdi par les voix de tout ce petit monde assemblé, cette confusion de la grande lumière qui faisait sous le lustre toutes les couleurs flottantes à force d'intensité, les rubans, les fleurs, les bruyères blanches des jardinières, les visages animés et souriants, tout m'est resté long-temps ainsi qu'un joli rêve avec le vague des choses reflétées, comme si, en entrant, j'avais vu le bal dans une glace, les yeux un peu troublés par l'heure de sommeil.

Indeed, Lemaître seems to be right. It is more of an impression than a picture . . .

> The sudden dazzle of the mirrors, the light. The piano muted, drowned by this single voice of an infant world, this confusion of blaze and bright-ness intensifying the colours floating underneath the chandelier, the ribbons, the flowers, the snowy heather in the *jardinières*, the faces, animated and

smiling, all of which remained in my mind for a long time like a happy dream, though with the haziness of things seen in reflection as if, when I entered the room, I had seen the dancers in a mirror with eyes already a little troubled by the first intimation of sleep.

Here is another extract:

Mais ce qui me charmait surtout, c'était de Musée ouvert sur les parterres, le *On ferme*! des gardiens vous précipitant des galères de peinture aux allées du jardin, à l'heure où le jour tombant rend aussi vagues les tableaux et les arbres, Quoique petite fille, on sortait de là avec je ne sais quelle attention aux choses d'art, une susceptibilité d'impressions qui vous faisait regarder les becs de gaz allumés dans la brume ou des paquets de violettes étalés sur un éventaire comme si on les voyait pour la première fois dans un Paris nouveau.

This charming notion of a childish mind seeing life through a haze of art, with a new susceptibility, 'when the falling day dims alike the pictures and the trees,' sharpens, on the contrary, one's image of Madame Daudet. This mind is, perhaps a little over-refined. It is the risk of every woman-writer, and then, especially, to be a lady-writer, to see writing as a decorative process,—not, indeed, for one would not be so cheap, of adornment like the adornment of the dressing-table but not, either, the search for that simplicity and harmony by which the Chinese reduce complexity to form and line—rather a process of 'being gracious,' even delicate-minded. She agreed herself that what she admired in literature was atmosphere and style.

How dangerously obtuse critics may be, under the influence of fashion, to the excellence of work that time puts *hors concours*! How easily they may divert a man from his real talent! That essay of Lemaître's on Madame Daudet illustrates this (and he is normally one of the most sure-footed of critics). It is puzzling in its failure to realize how wonderful those early stories of Daudet were; for while he admires them, he gives them a second place. For example, when it occurs to him to ask what role Julia Allard might have played in Daudet's life, the burthen of his answer is conditioned by the apparently accepted contemporary opinion that Daudet was not a short-story writer at all but a novelist.

> Without her Le Petit Chose would perhaps have gone on, all his life long, scribbling exquisite, fleeting fancies here and there at table-corners. She was to lead him, (le forcerait) to work without noticing that he was working. She was to induce him to write fine books (de beaux livres).

As if *Les Lettres de Mon Moulin* were a mere packet of trifles.

This is how he sees that happy marriage. Alphonse comes to Paris, all eager and thirsty, squandering his days, all the gifts of the gods, like a capricious young king scattering his treasures into the sea. She crosses his path.

> She has what it takes (se qu'il faut) to understand him: the most refined appreciation of beauty, a taste

wholly modern, an artist's imagination, and gifts of spiritual sanity and domestic virtue inherited from a family line well-buttressed by tradition and the rewards of honest industry.

(This, I presume, is a delicate-minded way of saying that she had money: he must, I begin to guess, have written this essay for the *Revue Bleu*, a highly refined periodical of the day.[1])

He continues:

She will take hold of him, wean him from bad influences, give him a dignified and happy home and, though younger than he, she will, for all that, be a mother to him. She will realize for him the dream of the poet[2] who, thinking of all the poor ailing artist souls of the world, said:

'Il leur faut une amie à s'attendrir facile
Souples à leurs vains soupirs comme aux vents de

roseau,

Dont le cœur leur soit un asile
Et les bras un berceau.

---

[1] Lemaître repeats all this, however, in his essay written at the death of Daudet. 'Transplanted from Nîmes to Lyons, he became Midi-conscious in that city of haze and, as I think, it gave him the capacity to become, one day, more than *un félibre superieur*. He comes to Paris, continues to squander his days and the gifts of the fairies, until a woman—his wife—takes him to her breast, at once calms and strengthens him and in bestowing on this gypsy the order and the peace of the home makes him capable of serious tasks and fine books.'
[2] Sully-Prudhomme.

'Douce, infiniment douce, indulgente aux chimères,
Inépuisable, en soins calmants ou rechauffants,
  Soins muets comme en ont les mères,
    Car ce sont des enfants.

'Il leur faut pour temoin, dans les heures d'étude
Une âme qu'autour d'eux ils sentent se poser ;
    Il leur faut une solitude
      Où voltige un baiser.'

She did collaborate with him directly in the making of those 'beaux livres,' now hardly read. Though the first novel, *Froment Jeune et Risler Aine*, has, I notice, just been reprinted in France, a high compliment in these days[1] when one may tramp all Paris without being able to buy a set of Maupassant or any but the better-known Stendhal. Daudet describes this process of collaboration and so does she. This is her account:

> Our collaboration was a Japanese fan. On one side was the subject, people, atmosphere; on the other, twigs, flower-petals, a frail branch lightly carried over with the last drops of paint, the last flecks of gold on the painter's brushes. It was I who performed these minute tasks, ever mindful of the main design on the obverse. . . .

He is more specific, in his Introduction[2] to *Froment Jeune et Risler Aîne*. He tells how he would talk with her over and over again about his work in progress.

[1] 1949.
[2] *Le Nouvelle Revue*, XIV, p. 361.

'What would you say to it if I made Sidonie die, eh? Suppose I let Risler live? What ought Delobelle, or Frantz, or Claire say on such and such an occasion?' And that would go on from morning to night, all the time, at meals, in the carriage, going to the theatre, coming back from a *soirée*, during those long journeys in cabs through the silence and the sleep of Paris. Ah! You poor wives of artists! It is the plain truth that mine is so much of an artist herself that she has been my partner in everything I wrote. Not a page that she has not checked, retouched, enriched with some of her lovely blue and gold. And yet so modest, so simple, so little about her of the 'literary woman.'

He describes how he would cover a page with writing, pass it to his collaborator, receive it back, copy it out in final form with infinite joy.

At either end of the immense room, my long table here, my wife's little desk there, and trotting between us, passing the copy from one to the other, my eldest boy[1] . . . with his thick blond curls falling on his little pinafore, black so as not to show the inkmarks of his first pothooks. It is one of the happiest memories of my life as a writer.

Nor was it only those conversations or these wifely emendations: if he wanted some difficult factual detail

---

[1] This is Léon Daudet, whose literary philosophy reacted violently away from his father's—certainly from that of his fathers group, the famous *auteurs stifflés*, Zola, De Goncourt, Flaubert and Turgenev.

he would, after the correct manner of the Zola-ist, go after it, direct to the source, with his family in train.

That dinner of Risler's and Sigismond's after the crash—I had that dinner myself, with my wife and son, at the Palais Royal, with the band playing.

No wonder Lemaître says:

Were he to attempt some risky subject, did he wish to describe some particularly shameful misery, modesty would restrain him, he would remain chaste because of her who watched him as he wrote . . . so that in all his work, even on those pages that bear the evident stamp of the great writer, even where she did not collaborate other than by her looks and her silent encouragement, one feels this diffused and delicate influence of a Beatrix who was always invisible—but always present.

All this is, once again, not about the exquisite short-stories but about the novels *Jack, Sapho, La Petite Paroisse, L'Evangeliste, Le Nabab, Les Rois en Exil, Nouma Roumestan* and *L'Immortel.*

I would not propose that Madame Daudet directly seduced Daudet away from Provence and his delicate meridional talent. There were, as we must see, all sorts of other and stronger influencés. Her love for style and atmosphere might, in fact, be expected to encourage that talent. Yet, one must remember that style and atmosphere convey to her chiefly—or so I feel—a sense of seemliness and propriety, and that, to her as to all Daudet's later friends he always appeared an unstable 'gypsy,' a wild woodland sprite, a Bohemian from the Brasserie des Martyrs, to be saved as G. K. Chesterton and Francis Thompson were to be 'saved.' Lemaître's reference to 'bad influences' is the remark of a *bien pensant* looking askance at such habitués of the Brasserie des Martyrs as Delvau and Murger and Baudelaire. Even De Goncourt and Flaubert seem to have felt that he needed to be stabilized. Once only, as far as I know, did Daudet feel the strain:

> 'Look here,' he cried to De Goncourt, 'it's most unfortunate. As a matter of fact you have upset me. Yes, you and Flaubert and my wife . . . I have no style. No, I have no, style, and that's the truth of it. People born on the other side of the Loire don't know how to write French prose. . . . What I was, was an *improvisatore*, a man of imagination. Well, but for you I should never have bothered myself about this brute of a language and I should have brought forth and brought forth in peace and quiet.'

He does not, as one sees, fully realize what they are doing to him. It is not just a question of language, alone. He is exactly right when he sees himself as 'an *improvisatore*,' bringing forth and bringing forth. R. H. Sherard, quoting this outburst in his memoirs of Daudet, interprets both better and worse, though we have to grant him, in excuse, that both Daudet and Madame Daudet were then still alive.

> Here we have, [he remarks] the cry of the cicada constrained to husbandry, the querulous complaint of *Le Petit Chose* brought back by the ear from Rhoneside

ramblings, and tied down to his desk, a complaint which is, in itself, the most eloquent testimony to the advantages which this writer has derived from his wife's influence.

They 'buckled me down' said Daudet, on another occasion, happily and gratefully.

3

Before tasting the quality of those novels it is to be said that there were, apart from this (highly suspect) influence of Julia Allard, precise reasons why Daudet allowed himself to be lured from the humour and tenderness that he had hitherto conjured like a mirage from the haze of Provence. For one thing his Provençal tales were far from popular when first published. The critics admired them. They failed to realize that, in those tales, they had before them a major achievement in French literature. This is something with which every writer of short-stories may expect to have to contend: that unless he also writes novels the public will not accept him as a major talent. His work, like the poet's talent, is select and must make its way slowly, like poetry, through a narrow channel of reputation. Maupassant, for example, is now regarded as a major French writer; the caution and condescension with which even Lemaître first wrote of him has to be read to be realized. (The moral of which is that no writer should pay the slightest attention to contemporary criticism.) There was also a special occasion in

Daudet's career that made him deliberately throw his more delicate talent overboard.

Three years after the publication of *Les Lettres de Mon Moulin* he saw his play *L'Arlésienne*, another Provençal piece, at the Vaudeville. The play was laughed off the stage. He tells us that he fled from the theatre, heartbroken, his ears red from the inane laughter of the audience at the emotional scenes, vowing that he would never again write for the stage, convinced that his Provençal vein was much too simple and too poetical for Parisian audiences. Yet, although the play was revived in his life-time with success, and is still played—it was staged in May 1947 at the Théâtre Francais, a more suitable venue than the junction of the grand boulevards before giggling and sceptical pleasure-seekers—it is hard to see much merit in it. It was a love-story of a highly sentimental and unpersuasive order, set in a farmyard, with comic opera decor, in silk and velvet, music by Bizet—musicians are familiar with the 'Suite Arlésienne'—the lights sinking for nightfall and rising for daybreak, with incongruous choirs chanting in the background, and it may well be the music rather than the play which attracts. The public had been right the first time. It is a silly play, and what Daudet should have concluded was not that there was some inherent lack of interest in the material, but that he was à short-story writer, and not a writer of plays. Instead he rushed home, pulled out another half-finished play and decided to recast it as a novel. It was *Froment Jeune et Risler Aîné*, which is about three hundred miles away from Aries and Arlésiennes. It was set in the Marais district of Paris, a quarter that had been fashionable in the eighteenth century, and was now given over to business and manufactures. He had some justification in choosing this background since his father had also been in the manufacturing business, in Lyons. The novel, alas, was a huge success. The public which had condescended to care for his stories lapped up this melodramatic picture of Parisian life. He decided that he had at last found his real *métier*—it was his talent to be another Zola. From that day novels of Parisian life poured from his pen.

4

Of the novels I find *Le Nabab* the most readable, or least unreadable, and I ought to say that Henry James considered *Numa Roumestan* 'a masterpiece'. But James is surely right in saying that in Daudet's other novels— and I would include this one—there is a 'perceptible tendency to the factitious.' If you tap them they sound hollow. They do not seem at all to have come from the same man who wrote the delicate short-stories of the South and of Paris in the seige, which bud and break as lightly as flowers on a stalk. The novels have the air of being built, *voulu*, acts of will-power, invented, sewn together. Zola said a fine thing about Daudet which hits off his weakness as a novelist. 'Benevolent nature has placed him at that exquisite point where poetry ends and reality begins.' And James has another phrase which exactly expresses the dilemma of such a talent: 'he pressed it a little hard.' That is, he pushed it forward from that 'exquisite point' where nature placed it into a realm beyond its scope. To illustrate I will take here but two examples, this first novel and *Le Nabab*, and make but two points.

Le Nabab is a chiaroscuro of an Algerian adventurer, six weeks in Paris when the novel opens. His barbaric wealth is lavished on all sides to forward his childish, uncontrolled ambitions. It leads him finally, but briefly, to a seat in the Chamber of Deputies from which he is ignominiously ejected for commercial frauds; he dies, melodramatically, while pleasure-seekers indifferently enjoy down-stairs the last of his largesse. This Jansoulet had a real prototype. Various other characters of Parisian life appear under disguised forms, including Daudet's patron, the Duc de Morny; it is said, Sarah Bernhardt; and the pivotal character, the Irish doctor, Jenkins, whose arsenical pills give temporary élan to the jaded frames of his wealthy clients, has been identified with a certain quack named Oliffe, who was probably originally a MacAuliffe. Other characters have been identified in the same way. To the public which first read this novel it had, therefore, a strong topical appeal—the Duc de Morny was only dead about thirteen years and the relatives of the prototype of Jansoulet were still there to object to Daudet's portrait. It seemed, furthermore, to the period, and to the critics of the decades immediately after Daudet's death, that the novel was guaranteed against the inherent danger of becoming 'dated' by its future permanent value as an historical document of the Second Empire, much as Balzac's novels have a (secondary) value as documents of an earlier period. Unfortunately a double fallacy undermines this opinion. Balzac exposed a whole society by his analysis of the types it produced. Daudet, essentially a short-story writer, concentrated on individuals, even on peculiar individuals, and his novel falls apart into a gallery of these separate portraits and of unconnected incidents. This is strikingly illustrated by the fact that a distinct short-story can be constructed, and has been constructed, out of the sewings and cuttings of three chapters in *Le Nabab*—'La Famille Joyeuse.'[1] Just as a short-story has been lifted out of *Les Rois en Exil* and called 'Chez le Médicin'. This episodic technique has been remarked over and over again by critics, and it is largely responsible for another outstanding weakness in Daudet as novelist, his love for melodramatic effects, inconceivable in the work of a man seeing his book as a whole, and relying on it as a whole for its comprehensive effect—i.e. inconceivable in a novelist though natural enough in a writer of *contes* or *nouvelles*. And it may be remarked, here, that even though other conditions tended to produce episodic or over-dramatic treatment, as for instance the obligations imposed by serial publication—*Froment* first appeared in serial form—yet veritable novelists have been able to build an all-over plan or theme, apparently outside Daudet's range, while working under exactly the same conditions: e.g. Dickens and Hardy.

One might fairly adopt the metaphor of the sprinter and the long-distance runner. The short-story writer likes to see the tape at the end of the sprint: he does not like the prospect of going round and round the course, or on and on over hedges and ditches, apparently getting nowhere. Set any short-story writer to work on a novel and he will inevitably break it up into episodes.

[1] See *Contes Choisies*. (Bibliothèque Verte. Hachette.)

Time and again as we read Daudet's novels we see this happening; as when the Irish doctor Jenkins enters the studio of the sculptress Félicia Ruys and catches the Nabab on the 'throne', passionately kissing her hand. At once he wins a round by declaring to the Algerian that a decoration is about to be bestowed on him, which causes him to rush from the studio; and wins the fight by telling Félicia that the fellow is married and has a large family. Whereupon the curtain falls on Félicia dashing the bust of the Nabab in ruin to the ground. It is embarrassingly violent, theatrical and unpersuasive, and in no wise in line with Daudet's naturally gentle talents. It is typical of much through-out his later books. What *is* in line with Daudet's talents is the delicate and tiny touch, all too rare, like:

'We have been at work since six o'clock this morning,' added the child with a rueful yawn which the dog caught on the wing, making him open wide his pink mouth with its sharp teeth.

But, as I shall have occasion to remark later on, there is normally no time for such delicate touches as these in the novel, whose vast sweep demands long strides and no delays. The novel and the short-story are two totally different genres and few men have been equally at home in both.

There is another point of distinction to be observed. The short-story is a more personal genre than the novel. It is the kernel of the matter on hand as the writer sees it. The writer need not be *explicit*; but we are likely to have much more difficulty in saying what knot a novelist ties or unties. It is this very characteristic of the short-story which has developed the technique of 'suggestion' rather than 'statement', a technique which is really an invisible cloak to cover the author, sensitive about intruding himself, fully conscious of the personal nature of his work, and just because he is so near at hand, for that very reason sensitive about being discovered prowling among his characters. No such sensibilities affected Daudet, the most eagerly personal of all writers, the charm of whose talent, as Henry James says, 'comes from its being charged to an extraordinary degree with his temperament, his feelings, his instincts, his natural qualities.' In the short-story Daudet could be as *personal* as he liked. It was his *métier.* But in the novel this personal intrusion has always been regarded as out of place, and is always resented by the reader. Daudet could *not* keep himself out of his novels. Only Dickens among novelists has intruded as blatantly as Daudet, and only a verve so immense can recompense for the habit. I think Daudet surpasses even Dickens in this. To quote James, again,

> Daudet is nothing if not demonstrative; he is always in a state of feeling; he has not a very definite ideal of reserve. . . . To be *personnel* to that point, transparent, effusive, gushing, to give oneself away in one's books has never been and never will be the ideal of us of English speech.

Nor, since Flaubert, can one say that it is an ideal of writers (or readers) in France or anywhere else.

Take the last scene of *Froment.* The main character of *Froment* is a minx, Sidonie Chèbe, explicitly said by

70

Daudet not to be a Bovary, yet deriving, I think, more than a little from her vicious romanticism. She is one of the poorest dwellers of the Marais, a friend of Clara Froment whose father owns the Wallpaper Factory of the Rue des Vieilles Haudriettes. Sidonie, devoured by ambition, jilts young Risler, is foiled in her scheme to marry George Froment—Clara marries him instead—and has to be satisfied with old Risler the designer, now Froment's partner. She becomes insensate with jealousy of Clara, wins her husband from her, ruins him and bankrupts the factory. It has to be confessed that when her husband, at last undeceived, drives her out of doors into the night, the snow is falling, and that as she flies in her ball-dress the dancers swirl heedlessly on. It has also to be confessed that he makes her go on her knees to Clara, having first stripped her. of her ill-gotten jewels, saying as he does so, 'On your knees! It must be! Restitution! Reparation! On your knees! Wretch!' She had earlier caught in her toils Frank Risler, her husband's brother, and extracted from him a love-letter which she finally shows to her husband. He has survived his wife's treachery, his brother's kills him. When he has duly hanged himself, his faithful old friend, Sigismond Planus, the cashier, brings down the final curtain by gazing out of the window at dawn breaking over Paris . . .

In the distance, far above Paris whose roar he heard but which he could not see, there rose a heavy and warm mist, moving sluggishly, touched at its rim with red and black like a cloud over a battlefield. Bit by bit, steeples, white façades, a golden cupola rose out of the mist, bursting forth at last in all the splendour

71

of the dawn. Then, a thousand factory chimneys, towering above this medley of clustered roofs, began to belch into the wind their panting smoke as feverishly as a steamer leaving a harbour. Life was beginning again! Onward machine! And so much the worse for those whom you leave behind!

At the sight, old Planus gave way to a movement of terrible indignation.

'Ah! You jade! You jade!' he cried, shaking his fist. And it was hard to say whether he was addressing the city—or the woman.

As a final outburst can one forgive the 'Onward, machine!' etc.? And if one compares it, say, with that last cold line of *Père Goriot* one quickly measures the chasm between the two writers. Perhaps Conrad has made the most just and generous comment on this demonstrative technique.

> But it is hard, [he says] it is sometimes very hard to forgive him the dotted i's, the pointing finger, this making plain of obvious mysteries. *Monsieur de Montpavon marche à la mort.* . . . We feel we cannot forgive until suddenly the naïveté of it all touches us with the revealed suggestion of a truth. Then we see the man is not false; all this is done in transparent good faith. The man is not melodramatic; he is only picturesque [Conrad, however, concludes]—His characters' fate is poignant; it is intensely interesting; and of not the slightest consequence.

How can it be? It is Daudet whom we like, it is Daudet who comes out best of all the farrago; the kind Daudet who cries, aghast at the wickedness of his own Sidonie, 'But in this venal little mind the first kiss of love had only given birth to plans of ambition and luxury!'; who cries, in boyish delight, when her first lover comes back to expose her, 'Frank Risler thinks only of avenging the honour of the Rislers. He comes not as a lover but an avenger! And Sidonie must beware!' It is of his awe that we are aware, not of the awe of the situation, when the deceived husband meets the man who has betrayed him, and the author cries, with a grip on our arm, a pointing finger and rolling eyes—'The first few minutes of that meeting were *terrible!*' This writer who is, and so effectively, self-exposing and self-giving in the stories, still touches us; but Conrad and James are right—in the tales, where he is so much part of the emotion, we are one with him; in the novels the factitious contrivances stand between.

5

Daudet's surrender to the modish Naturalism is a warning to every writer to be suspicious of his milieu. Let us pursue the trail further into the general history of the idea of Naturalism; first taking a swift view of the whole terrain of this subject of Realism and Naturalism in fiction, most easily considered, for the moment, in the Novel. We can then close in on Daudet's personal dilemma.

What is realism, simply? Realism (without the capital letter) has always been found in literature. Every writer of fiction wishes to convey, in some fashion, an illusion of reality. It is an elementary part of his task to overcome his reader's natural disinclination to treat, for the moment, as physical fact what is a mere arrangement of words. In this the novelist differs from the poet in so much as the poet does not generally wish to be as representational as the novelist, is not so eager to make a photograph with words. The poet dominates the imagination by transporting us out of the physical world into a more 'insubstantial existence' where words and images become hierophantic. He intoxicates us into that realm with a swirl of eloquent sound and imagery that is not, as a rule, so much descriptive as suggestive. '*The fat weed that rots itself in ease on Lethe's wharf*', is not a picture of an actual botanical process. One cannot take literal meanings out of the individual words in even so simple a poem as—

> *Sweet Highland Girl, a very shower*
> *Of Beauty is thy earthly dower;*
> *Twice seven consenting years have shed*
> *Their utmost beauty on thy head. . . .*

It is only by a series of conventions, slowly developed over centuries, that we understand the connotation of those lines, although, of course, we have grown up so naturally in those conventions that we now have long ceased to realize how conventional they are, and find no difficulty in understanding the idea that 'years' can 'consent' to anything. But if we were children again we would. And if a child could be educated without reference to the hundred-and-one conventions of poetry it would, if it grew to be a writer, either write quite literally, or, such being the natural urge to transcend reality, it would invent conventions of its own to express

74

its imaginations. Thus my small daughter, when aged eleven, saw no oddity in her first efforts at writing verse in saying that the rising sun got on a chair to look at the world. And this is to make no mention at all of the language of the actual *metre* itself, which is such a vast imbroglio of conventions that only the really cultivated critic can translate them fully.

The novelist employs less of those conventions, being more anxious to dominate the senses and the mind than to excite the imagination. His method, I do not say his object, is to create the illusion that we are having actual, physical experiences of all the senses. This, of course, is itself another colossal convention or series of conventions of which it is enough that the dictionary definition of fiction equates it with 'a conventionally accepted falsehood'—the falsehood being, primarily, but not wholly, that the human reason is mesmerized into accepting that a description of a sensation is a sensation. Thus when we read that 'Henry sighed' these words are not words but Henry and his sigh, and indeed, by sympathy, we partake of the existence of Henry and his sigh—we are Henry sighing.

The further intellectual and imaginative experience which we share is what makes a novel a moral 'experience' and not merely a physical 'experience'. This is where we come up against the distinction between Realist and Naturalist novels.

The total *object* of the novelist, of any writer, of any artist, cannot be merely to create an illusion of physical reality. If that were so the cinema gives a better illusion than any painter or any writer could ever hope to give. The illusion of physical reality cannot be more than a technique towards a larger end. On that Henry James has a good passage in which he compares the novel to an orange which one squeezes for the juice, and so often, when we read and read and read through some long novel it is like squeezing a dummy orange—you have all the appearances, the texture, the illusion, the colour, the lifelikeness—but where is the juice? As we might say today, having read these empty novels one is inclined to ask, 'So what?'. A novel, says Henry James, changing his image, is a monument; but it is a monument to something. Had he known Ireland and seen those many curious monuments which kindhearted people erected during the Famine to give employment, all deliberately non-functional and irrelevant, lest this cheap labour compete with regular labour, he might have compared those empty novels to those empty monuments. Empty novels also give employment to cheap labour, and the public visits these meaningless monuments of a hundred years ago in much the same vacant, undemanding spirit that it approaches the unrewarding fictions of today.

This is equally true of the 'realistic novel'. It was Brunetière who said, speaking of the technique of Realism, that is merely *un tremplin*—a spring-board. From the illusion there leaps whatever the novelist has in his heart to make leap. To use a loose word, some generalization emerges; not, indeed, some close-packed moral (Heaven forbid!); not even, of necessity, something capable of definition—rather an attitude, a characteristic mood, a sudden wash of colour drawn across the landscape of experience. Where the realistic novel broke new ground was in the greater hardihood of its generalizations, the challenge of its colouring. The sentimental novelist's generalizations about life and society once lay in the mere vicissitudes of the hero and heroine; or rather in their inevitable conclusion, which the reader awaited with a barely-shaken imperturbability—as when in a melodrama one is only pleasantly disturbed at seeing the circular-saw approach the body of the heroine. Love was thwarted, but it came right in the end; the good were inevitably rewarded; the wicked inevitably slunk away—as in *The Vicar of Wakefield*, which was the Novel barely beginning to break away from the sentimental convention. Partly due to the fact that the charm of these ingenuous devices of suspended *dénouement* became exhausted by habit, and partly because literature ceased gradually to be the titillation of the privileged classes, these pretty imaginary worlds began to disappear out of the Realistic Novel. The rise of the middle-classes in the eighteenth century gave them a right to a place in literature, both as readers and writers. An early effect was the novels of Jane Austen. The emancipation of the poor followed slowly, and as these gradually began to take a larger and larger place in literature, the romantic view of life died. There were other influences to which we must return à propos of Daudet and Maupassant.

One small result, for example, was the disappearance of the pleasant convention that 'they lived happily ever after'. Love was treated much more circumstantially. Once it had inevitably led to marriage, and that was the end of the story. The realists did not *know* better, in this regard, than the romantics; but they did have the courage to say some things that the sentimental novelist knew but could not bear to admit. And when the *Quarterly* reviewed *Emma* it strongly protested against this insult to 'Cupid', and warned the new school that they might, at this rate, for all their honesty, thereby induce many more mean and sordid and selfish motives than the romantics did with their fairy-tales. Which is a sufficiently intriguing defence for telling lies to have been invented by Gilbert Chesterton. For it was not at first realized that Realism had its own high morality. The lesson of Balzac's *Père Goriot* (1834), which may be taken as the classic of Realism, could not be bettered by a Redemptorist preacher. Accepted codes in their fundamentals were always present. Virtue might not be rewarded—Is it in Life?—but if it was not, neither was wickedness.

But the novelists were not yet satisfied. There were still inherent conclusions even in the Realistic Novel which they questioned, and conventions which they disliked. They said that, in practice, life does not round to *any* conclusion. The novel of actual existence does not end with page 365. Some romantic trappings, such as plot, counterplot, the oppositions of good men and bad men, the Missing Letter, the Overheard Conversation, the Happy Coincidence, the moral assumptions, the conventional solutions, were further lies to be eradicted without pity. To this end there arose keywords, or slogans, such as 'exact anatomy', 'human documents', 'experimental novel' to indicate that, in future, for everything stated in a novel there must be, as far as possible, scientific proof. The influence of nineteenth century scepticism and positivism is apparent here, as it is apparent that, in praising science, in demanding facts and in assailing the imagination, what the new school was really doing was denying that there was any mystery in life, any inexplicable miracle at all.

The premise on which the new 'naturalistic' novel was based was philosophical determinism. The man who most ruthlessly formulated it was Daudet's friend Zola. And he had no doubt where Daudet stood.

> My literary friends' . . . opinion on literary matters is the same as mine in every respect. . . . I am only the younger brother of Flaubert and of De Goncourt just as I am the brother-in-arms of Daudet.

The classical statement of the theory of Naturalism in fiction is Zola's 'Le Roman Experimental'. This is one of a series of articles which Zola contributed at Turgenev's instigation to the *Messager de l'Europe* of Saint Petersburg in 1875. (Zola began to write for this review when the French papers were afraid to touch him: the *Corsaire* had just then been suppressed owing to an article of his.) It is to be noted, however, that this is a very late date in the history of Naturalism. Zola himself had been issuing the Rougon-Macquart series since 1869, and he is quite right in saying, as he did, that he invented nothing new. Flaubert's *Madame Bovary*, the classic of Naturalism, had appeared in 1857. De Goncourt's *Germinie Lacerteux* had studied the life of the common people in characteristic fashion in 1865. It had all been there before him: all he did was to take to their logical and often absurd conclusions, ideas that had been in the air for years.

It is usual to treat 'Le Roman Expérimental' super-
ciliously; to say, in effect, 'Of course, there is really
nothing at all in this nonsense of Zola's.' When anybody makes this sort of remark about a popular idea
one may be sure that the idea is firmly established.
It is as if one said today, 'Really does psychoanalysis
tell us as much about human nature as is commonly
imagined?' And when, around 1884, Jules Lemaître
said about psychology in fiction, in the course of an
essay on Maupassant 'Really, this business of psychology in fiction is overdone', we may take it as a date
at which the mechanics of Naturalism have become
an accepted technique. That there is a good deal of
force in Zola's 'Le Roman Expérimental' is proved
by the fact that all subsequent writers of fiction, even
men and women who probably have never read a line
he wrote, faithfully follow his precepts. In our day,
it seems to me, his method is almost universally and
disastrously triumphant.

Zola based his exposition of his literary theories
on the writings of Claude Bernard (1813-1878), a
physiologist of genius whose *Introduction à la médicine
expérimentale* has been compared to the *Discours sur
la Méthode* of Descartes. In sum Bernard applied to
living creatures the technique of physics: i.e. clinical
and controlled observation, followed by a hypothesis to interpret what the observer has dispassionately
recorded, rounded off by the verification of this
hypothesis by experiment. By this method he discovered the sugar-making secretion of the liver and the
vasomotor system of the nerves. Zola was entranced
by this rational approach to the study of the human
organism, and saw in it a clear parallel for the study of

human character. An experiment, he. said, is merely an observation which one has been provoked to make. An experimental novel is merely something which one has been provoked to write in order to test and prove a national hypothesis. 'It is the official report of an experiment (the *procès-verbal*) read in public.' Just as a scientist submits his subjects to certain tests to prove his theory, so the novelist will move his characters this way and that to show that the succession of incidents will be that which is dictated by the determination of the phenomena which he is studying. Thus, in Balzac's *Cousine Bette*, we have a temperamentally amorous man, Baron Hulot, submitted to certain tests, or incidents, to show us how the mechanism of his passion functions. This is the 'Roman Experimental'. It is, in Zola's words, the novelist continuing the work of the physiologist.

Zola was quite aware that it would be pointed out to him that the human liver is an inert, obedient mass without a will which reacts passively to experiments, whereas man has a will of his own and, being free, is therefore unpredictable. His answer to that was not that he did not believe in the will but that he believed more in the milieu. 'Le déterminisme,' he said, categorically, 'domine tout.' There is an external milieu and there is an internal milieu, or 'mechanism of the passions', and once these are granted, stated and measured, everything must inevitably follow. To those who said that he must therefore be a fatalist he replied that, on the contrary, fatalists suppose that things manifest themselves independently of conditions, whereas his stress was all on the conditions. If anybody declared that his theory was a doctrine of hopelessness he replied, warmly, that to master good and evil, to regulate life and society, to resolve all the problems of socialism, to erect a solid basis for justice by solving problems of criminality according to experimental techniques was to do the most useful and moral work possible; and he poured scorn on the so-called idealists who 'take refuge in the Unknown for the mere pleasure of it'.

He was equally aware that it would be pointed out to him that every novelist is subject to his own personal quality of mind and nature, so that no observer could ever be utterly objective. This, he asserted, was the whole point of the experimental idea, and he quoted Bernard to the effect that the nature of the observer and of his theories must, inevitably, be quite individual. 'C'est un sentiment particulier un *quid proprium* qui constitue l'originalité, l'invention, ou le génie de chacun.' It is the essence of the theory that the observer will doubt and doubt, will remain quite free-minded and sceptical, and only cease to doubt when he sees that the 'mechanism of the passions, having been taken to bits and put together again, still functions according to the laws of its nature'. So the novelist, willy-nilly, must continue the work of the physiologist, reducing all things to responsive machines (*rouages obéissants*). The experimental method alone proclaims liberty of thought without any *parti pris*.

Granted his own *parti pris*, his theory is unassailable. That the results, as novels, must also be intensely boring he and his successors down to our own time have demonstrated perfectly. The only other fault I have to find with his theory is not, as has been said, that he took a moderate idea too far but that he did not take it far enough: it would be the logical conclusion that the physiologist should so operate on the living organism, on, for example, the brain of Zola, that it would be directed like a *rouage obéissant* to create fiction to order. Lyrics, novels and short-stories painlessly extracted. Alternatively we might have a moral novel about the major gut. An intestinal tract.

It is interesting that it was not Zola the inexorable Naturalist but Balzac the moderate Realist whom Engels acclaimed, saying that from his novels he had 'learnt more (about French society from Napoleon to' 48) than from all the professed historians, economists and statisticians of the period put together'. And this was the Balzac who had proclaimed himself 'a monarchist, a legitimist and a Catholic'.

Zola naturally chose the material most suitable to his theory—laying, for example, much stress on the social milieu, and on heredity. One of his Rougon-Macquart novels deals with the life of Les Halles: he called it *Le Ventre*—the belly of Paris. (He did not disregard the major gut.) Another novel studies the life of the railways; a third, art-life; a fourth, the life of the big shops; another, the life of the peasants. Naturally, too, his people tend to move in great masses, as in *Germinal*, where the miners come out on strike. He loves, too, to give life to inanimate things. When he read, with keen pleasure, a description in Daudet's *Jack* of a steam-engine being hoisted aboardship as if it were a struggling, panting, living thing, it seems to have suggested to him the idea of making a steam-pump in *Germinal* also pant and strain as if it were alive. Not unnaturally, also, his people refuse to be *rouages obéissants* and take on urges of their own, independently of conditions and in defiance of his own deterministic philosophy. Thus, M. Denis Saurat observes[1] that the same Jean who is a stupid dumb beast in *La Terre*—as a peasant might be clinically supposed to be, in his conditions—becomes 'brave, sensible and effective in *La Débâcle* (Zola's novel about 1870) where the war makes a man of him although it is a calamity and a failure'. Is one to draw some 'provoked observation' from this about war in general? And, if so, what is it? That peasant-life brings out the beast in men, but that war brings out the man in what, before it, was a beast? This may be quite true, or it may not. The doubt indicates the weakness of the Naturalistic or experimental theory since it means that two novelists, with opposing hypotheses, might quite, easily show their characters behaving in opposite ways under similar conditions. What is really at work here, however, as M. Saurat has also pointed out, is Zola's (unwilling) sense of the miraculous. He cannot deny that there are inexplicable flashes of goodness and beauty in all men; the artist in him sweeps aside his theories to insist on it. 'Zola has suppressed God but he has scattered the divine qualities all over his human material, and among the worst something which seems to be festering is really germinating. The forces are at work, and their movement is upwards.' Again we may agree, while gently asking of the shade of Zola, 'What forces?'

[1] *Modern French Literature*, 1870-1941, Denis Saurat, London 1946.

6

Now, what was Daudet, the gentle poet of Provence, doing in this deterministic *galère?* Why did he think he belonged here? I think the answer is that Daudet was a rather simple soul; frank, spontaneous, eager as a boy, enthusiastic and generous beyond limits, very trusting, easily influenced. He also wanted success, as who does not. His nature, his ambition and his milieu combined to persuade him that this was the proper way to write *de beaux livres.*

Whatever went into Daudet had to come out. When he was younger his simple, natural self had simply and naturally responded to the attraction of the South, and he wrote of it, with infinite care and artistry. When he came up to Paris he still went on, for a time, writing about Provence, still went back there—to that old windmill which he made famous. When he went, for his health, to Corsica, he wrote, on his experiences there, those unforgettable impressions, *Le Phare des Sanguinaires* and *L'Agonie de la Semillante.* When he was poor in Paris he haunted the bohemian cafés around Notre Dame de la Lorette, drinking and idling with, to mention from among those scores of wasted lives, a few names that have survived, Murger, Malassis, Dupont, Alfred Delvau, and, the greatest of them all, Baudelaire. And as it went in so it came out—in *Jack* and in his memoirs. When he married and was climbing the ladder, at the time of his first novel, he belonged to the group calling themselves *les auteurs sifflés,* Flaubert, Zola, De Goncourt, Turgenev. This was to move in the very heart of naturalism. The influences were too much for him.

He was touchingly imitative. Thus it is sad to see Daudet, like Zola, compiling mountains of facts in piles of notebooks: as he made use of an item he would strike it out with a coloured pencil lest he should use it again. It was merely comical to see him imitating Barbey D'Aurevilly's dandy's clothes. It is rather charming when he refuses the Duc de Morny's appeal to cut his hair. It is odd to see this naturally sanguine creature buckling down to his big books. ('There is too much paper in it,' Flaubert said of *Jack.*) It is most of all revealing to find him buried in the modish gloom.

Lemaître is good on this, for, as he truly says, gloom is inherent in Zola, it is part of his nature, his philosophy, the colouring of his mind, it is internal; whereas in Daudet one does not feel that this is so. The passage is well worth quoting at length, for all that he says equally needs to be said today: it might be called 'In defence of the Happy Ending':

> If the rest of a man's book, however sad it be, does not imply a philosophy of complete negation and despair; if the ferocity of the dénouement is not forced on him by the logic of his subject and the nature of his own mind, I fail to see what aesthetic advantage there is in the writer's constant and systematic refusal to yield to the universal feeling that the good should be rewarded. What, in brief, I reproach Daudet for is a tendency to force pity, a pessimism which is not innate in this happy Provençal, but to which he buckles himself—and

86

which, moreover, he frequently forgets. . . . The novels of Zola are pessimistic *au fond*, internally pessimistic. It is vain for him to make the action and dénouement of his books other than tragic. From beginning to end we are left with a feeling of disgust, a black melancholy which leaves our eyes dry—and thereby sins against the light all the more.

When misery is held to be irresponsible, pity declines into bitterness. There is no reason to believe that Daudet had any philosophy of irresponsibility, and in such bitterness as we find in his novels he was lightly false to everything that he essentially was. It is not just that the solemn personality he created for himself as a novelist was factitious—all created literary personalities partake of this: it is that it bore such little relation to his talents. So, the truth is that he could not compass bitterness, he could not be farouche, his gloom is fake-gloom and does not impress us: the natural sweetness and goodness of his nature defeats him, or, may one say, saves him, as Conrad, by the percipient generosity of his own nature, was able to see. It is not pleasant when Zola perceives this in another way, noting that one still entangled in idealism and poetry seems destined by Providence, and his feminine charms, to lead to the new literature souls whom human documents *tout crus* would frighten off completely. As it transpired it has worked the other way round. Daudet's novels are readable for their Daudet-ism; unreadable for their Zola-ism. They can only remind us of another sort of *cru*—the good Rhône wine of the stories of his true nature.

For writers and philosophers, in the end, do not, as Emile Faguet has said in a most charming and civilized essay on 'La Tristesse Contemporaine', produce current ideas: they reflect current feelings. The gloom of Zola is not Zola's gloom: it is a reflection of a contemporary melancholy, creeping into life for many generations, at least since the revolution hoped impossible hopes and science dreamed impossible dreams of perfectibility, all proven less likely than they at first seemed. But neither is Daudet's gloom the gloom of Daudet; nor is it the gloom of Zola which was not Zola's; nor is it the gloom which Zola reflects; his gloom is just a bad joke. The man was a happy man. He loved people; he loved life, *as it is*; he accepted, he rejoiced, he was a gentle Pantagruelist. Just because he was so happy he put on a mask and growled Fee-fo-fum. We are not frightened. We can see the happy eyes of *le petit chose*. Besides, as Faguet well says, this current gloom, was largely the 'misères des grands seigneurs': the mass of men did not feel it profoundly; the current feeling was confined to the lords of fortune and of thought. Daudet was not one of those—he was a good fellow, he was a simple fellow, he was a very normal and natural fellow, or, as I said in the beginning he was simply a local boy who made good.

7

These are the two outstanding characteristics of his short-stories, an almost greedy happiness, and the tears of that supreme happiness. It has been suggested indeed that the apple in his Eden was his discovery that the most extraordinary thing in the world was the world itself: that because he could not be content any longer to look at life he ate it: i.e. that because he rejoiced in its fantasy he fell in love with its reality—and was fool enough to call it Realism.

The stories tell of such *little* things, things almost fanciful, so light and slight they are. They are not things that anybody could have observed deliberately. They have been felt as a child feels, with intensity. (Zola, had no such remembering, feeling eye. To a friend when writing *Nana*:—'Oh, by the way I forgot. I shall want an exact, scientific and very detailed description of the death-mask of a woman who died of common smallpox. Thanks in advance.') Indeed with Daudet fancy and observation are one act. It is this which makes analysis of his work impossible: to take them to pieces is like pulling a flower apart, it is his personality which one would pull apart.

Take up 'Les Vieux'. It opens with a letter from Paris, received at the mill. It is a letter as odd as a Phiz drawing, only more kind, and more shot with poetry.

'You must do me a favour, old chap. You must shut your mill for a day and go off to Eyguières at once. It's a big market-town about seven or eight miles from you—just a pleasant walk. When you get there ask for the orphanage. The first house after that is a lowbuilt house with gray shutters and a little back-garden. Go in, without knocking—the door is always open; and as you walk in shout out, very loud, "Hello, folks! I'm Maurice's pal." Then you'll see two little old people, Oh, so old, so very old, as old as old, stretching up their hands to you from the depths of their big armchairs and you'll kiss them for me, with your whole heart, as if they were your own people. Then you'll chat, and they'll talk to you about me, all the time about me, and they'll tell you a thousand silly nonsensical things that you must listen to without a smile. . . . Not a smile, remember! . . . They're my grandparents, those two. I'm the whole world to them. They haven't seen me for ten years. . . . Ten years! Yes, it's a long time, but hang it, I'm stuck in Paris and they're so old. They're so old that if they came here to see me they'd crumble into little bits on the way. However, by great good luck you're down there, my dear old miller, and when they kiss you the poor old things will imagine they're kissing a bit of me. I've talked such a lot to them about us two and the lovely friendship which . . .' The devil fly away with him and his friendship . . .

And so on. And the devil fly away with the word 'charm' that comes at once to one's pen, for what is it to say 'charm' but to say 'alchemy'.

Touch upon touch does it. The fine day, his nook in the rocks where he lies like a lizard and listens to the pines, his key put into the cat's hole—there is one intimate *remembered* detail—and his pipe, and his stick and the long dusty road to Eyguières. It is the details that do it but is the heart which remembers that really does it.

All my life long I'll be seeing that long corridor, so cool and fresh, the high walls pink-washed, and at the end the little garden quivering at me across a luminous windowblind, and on all the door-panels fading flowers and violins. . . . At the end of this corridor, on the left, through a half-open door, the tick-a-tock of a grandfather clock and a child's voice, a schoolgirlish voice, reading, halting at every syllable. 'And there . . . up . . . on . . . Saint . . . Ir . . . en aeus . . . excl . . . aimed . . . I . . . am . . . the . . . wheat . . . of . . . the . . . Lord . . . I approached the door very quietly and looked in. In that calm and demi-dusk of a tiny room I see an old chap, with two rosy cheeks, wrinkled to the tips of his fingers, asleep in the deeps of an armchair, his mouth open, his hands lying on his knees. At his feet sits a little girl dressed in blue, with a big cape and a little cap, the orphange uniform, and she is reading the *Life of Saint Irenaeus* from a tome as big as herself. The legend had laid its fingers on its lips. The old man slept in his chair, the flies slept on the ceiling, the canaries slept in their cage in the window. The great clock snored, *Tick-a-tock, tick-a-tock.* Nothing was awake in the room but a great wide band of sunlight shooting straight and clear between the closed shutters, brilliant with dancing flecks and waltzing atoms.

Not all the notebooks in the world could contain one detail of that; nothing but a memory moist with tears of joy. But what pains, what care, or else what 'natural selection' must have been at work: as one soon learns when one tries to render in English a line like 'le jardinet qui tremblait au fond à travers un store de couleur claire'. This is the language of poetry on loan to prose.

This is, also, humour so delicate that the pattern is faint on the plate. A light touch laid it on, it is already ancient, already classic, it will never fade, it will always be faint, like the smell of bergamot from the old cupboard where the cherries-in-brandy were hidden. They had been waiting there ten years for the selfish Maurice, and now his friend must broach it.

In spite of the appeals of Mamette the old chap insisted on going after the cherries himself and, mounted on the chair, to the terror of his wife, he was trying to reach up to them. . . . You see it? The old man tremblingly stretches upward, the two little blue-coated girls clutch the chair, Mannette stands behind him, panting, her arms upward, and over it all there hangs the frail perfume of bergamot from the open cupboard and the great layers of russet linen.

(Why russet, I have always wondered.) But I must add what Daudet cannot refrain from adding—'C'était charmant.' (Like Madame de Stael's 'C'est joli, une feuille qui chante.') How easily it could all be too *charmant*. But Daudet is either clever by art or by nature, for he lays his irony besides his sentiment to salt it. You remember? The cherries had not been sweetened. 'Elles étaient atroces, vos cerises, ma pauvre Mamette.' He ate them to the end without a grimace.

How does it end, this islet of reality conjured from the haze of Provence, a mirage, a little dream of delight? One must return to one's mill. The old man must, to prove himself a man, walk some of the way with his guest, though on his arm. The little child in blue creeps after them, unseen, to lead him back, so proud, unseeing, of being a man, still' Mamette, beaming, saw his pride from the doorstep and as she watched us her chin nodded and nodded as much as to say, "All the same, my poor old man can walk still!" ' And there the little masterpiece ends. For if it is not a little masterpiece, worth all the long fat books that Daudet ever wrote, then literature and criticism are bedlamites, and we can all go and boil our heads and stop writing.

Of what *is* it composed? As Lemaître says—truth, fancy, wit, tenderness, gaiety, melancholy, all in one little tale. 'There is no plot!' the editor may say. 'It is nice but slight', the writer of yarns may say. 'There is no psychology', the realist may say. 'It is a little thing', the novelist may say. 'The best and most pleasing writers,' Montesquieu says, 'are those who excite in the soul the greatest number of simultaneous sensations.'

What delights us in those tales, too, is not only the unanalysable quality of the technique alone but the unmodern *lightness* of his personality. The very choice of subject is so old and, one might say, traditional; as simple as Theocritus. He should have delighted George Moore, who loathed the moralizing of the moderns, that mark of intellectual malady which Faguet calls the ransomprice of our latter-day sense of superiority, and of which we have made the poisonous pastry we call 'serious literature'. Today young men choose for subjects the most enormous and monstrous themes. A pair of old children like 'Les Vieux' would seem beneath them, effeminate, unserious. But we all like labour in our day! And Lemaitre is right, charm and labour do not lie together; and Daudet proved it when he 'buckled down', for in his labour his charm was to die. But that is a modern curse, too, to want to *faire grand* before one is able to make at all. No subject is

93

too small for genius. M. Séguin's goat; M. Cornelle's empty mill; two inns, one empty the other full; a child idling on the river (that delightful thing, 'Le Pape est Mort'); an old monk making wine (that perfect story 'L'Elixir du révérent Père Gaucher'); a starry night.

Daudet is a pagan in that he begins with his senses and ends with his heart, and his mind would seem sound asleep if all his being were not so evidently awake. But that was where we came in, was it not? That by technique we cannot mean tricks but an art that is not much learned as practised—practised for us, perhaps, by race, by tradition, by our blood, but, naturally, as far as we ourselves are concerned, practised chiefly by ourselves: the art of fully being. It is in the putting of ourselves to work that the difficulties begin, for few writers are so lucky as Daudet as to be unaffected and unselfconscious, and to have subjects in concordance with this, their awakened being, ready to hand, and, though so poor, to have so much courage, and to be so blessedly ignorant of the world, and of fame, and publishers, and critics, or, when these must be met, few so lucky as to meet editors like Villemessant of *Figaro*. For sooner or later the world says, 'Do come in, little writer!' And then, as happened to poor Daudet in the end, indeed so soon, we may never get out of the parlour again.

ANTON CHEKOV
OR *THE PERSISTENT MORALIST*

Russian novelists are more stupid than their readers, their heroes are wan and insignificant, and the life they treat is bare and uninteresting. A Russian writer lives in the gutter and eats woodlice, loves frowsy women and laundresses, knows nothing of history or geography or natural sciences, and is ignorant of the religion of his native land, its administration and its legal procedure . . . in a word he knows absolutely nothing.

CHEKOV to SOUVORIN 15 May, 1889

He who desires nothing, hopes for nothing, and is afraid of nothing, cannot be an artist.

CHEKOV to SOUVORIN
25 November 1892

While preparing to write this book I again re-read all Chekov's tales. I began, casually, with his 'Verotchka'. It was years since I had read it because I had for long had a feeling that it is just a dreamy, romantic, pretty, atmospheric tale, with a lovely scenery of mists over the fields under the moon—that and no more. Having re-read it I feel, once again, that nobody should read more than he can in ten years re-read; that first reading is a pleasure for youth, second reading an instruction for manhood, and third reading, no doubt, the consolation and despair of old age. For 'Verotchka' re-read is simply another thing altogether.

Do you remember 'Verotchka'? All I got from it in my youth was that a young man, Ognev, goes to the country and meets an old man and his pretty daughter, Vera or Verotchka. Leaving them, he walks away from the house through the moonlit fields, full of fine sentiments:

> He walked along thinking how frequently one met with good people, and what a pity that nothing was left of those meetings but memories. At times one catches a glimpse of cranes on the horizon, and a faint gust of wind brings their plaintive ecstatic cry, and a minute later, no matter how greedily one scans the blue distance, one cannot see a speck nor catch a sound: and like that, people, with their faces and their words flit through our lives and are drowned in the past, leaving nothing except faint traces in the memory.

Then Verotchka comes towards him and they talk, and she does not seem to want to leave him and he wonders why and he talks about never having had a romance, and drools on and on about how they will, perhaps, meet in ten years' time and not have a memory of one another. Suddenly she blurts out that she loves him so they need never part. He is aghast, and confesses that he does not love her, and she hurries away from him. His fine sentimental bubble is burst; and he thinks that something precious is lost to him, part of his youth never to be repeated. He goes back to the house, looks at it, sighs, throws up his hands, and goes away.

It is the father of a hundred imitative Chekov-stories of our day, but the imitators have either harshened it with a cruder Naturalism, or diluted it with rose-water sprinkled with cherry-blossoms. They have not noticed the sentence:

> For the first time in his life it was his lot to learn by experience how little that a man does depends on his own will, and to suffer in his own person the feelings of a decent, kindly man who has against his will caused his neighbour cruel, undeserved anguish.

They have missed the ironic detachment; and, above all, that this is one of the most frequent subjects of Chekov—the motif most often heard from beginning to end, sometimes satirized in his so kindly way that it can hardly be called satire (as in *The Three Sisters*)— the frustration that descends on the sentimental mind which deceives itself, which evades reality, and which ultimately breeds lies, smugness and cant. They have who imitate merely the romantic atmosphere failed to see that there is here a quality of *mind* that is always in Chekov, controlling his emotions, so that he does not bathe in the thing, but contemns it all while he writes of it so sensitively—an approach which is uniquely his own. Later he developed, with greater strength this motif and this approach in 'The Wife' (1892; frustration and self-deception); 'Gooseberries' and 'About

97

Love' (1898; lies and smugness); 'Ionitch' (1898) or 'Excellent People' (sham; the neurotic sentimental male and female).

One could really write a book on Chekov with no other illustration than this story 'Verotchka'—which would be printed in the first few pages, and referred to throughout. It was published in his third volume of stories, in 1887 (he was born in 1860), the first book to bring him any reputation—including the Poushkin Prize. With it were 'At Home', 'The Witch', 'A Trifling Occurrence', 'On the Road' and 'A Nightmare'.[1] Before that he had been writing for the comic papers, without regard for his talent, merely to earn a few roubles for clothes and food: then had come Gregorovitch's letter of encouragement in 1886 and the essential Chekov began to show himself. In embryo that essential Chekov is in 'Verotchka'.

One thing he is always saying is—'I hate violence and falsehood in all their aspects.'

I detect them in science, in religion, in the younger generation. For these reasons I have no partiality for gendarmes, or butchers, or savants, or writers, or the younger generation. I look upon labels and trade-marks as prejudices. My Holy of Holies is the human body, health, mind, talent, inspiration, love, and the most absolute freedom—freedom from violence and falsehood in whatever they may be manifested.

Again he speaks of the framework of a novel he is planning as 'the absolute freedom of man, freedom

[1] The references are to the Constance Garnett translations.

from violence, from prejudices, from ignorance, the devil, freedom from passions, etc'.

This gospel of normality informs a great deal of his work as well as his life, and one cannot say too emphatically that Chekov's work was the affirmation of normality. 'Dinner at the Continental,' he enters in his diary, 'to commemorate the anniversary of the great reform (abolition of serfdom). Tedious and absurd. To dine, drink champagne, make a noise, deliver speeches about the national consciousness, the conscience of the people, freedom and such things, whilst slaves in tailcoats are running round your tables, veritable serfs, and your coachmen wait outside, in the street, in the bitter cold—that's lying to the Holy Spirit.' The same earnest spirit gives us the bitter mocking laughter of 'The Grasshopper'—taken direct from life with, as models, the painter Levitan and a Moscow lady of his acquaintance, both presented so veritably that Chekov nearly incurred a libel action over it. It gives the fire of honest loyalty to his stories of such simple decent people as the provincial doctors in 'The Princess', 'The Wife', 'A Doctor's Visit', or the priest in 'Nightmare'. It gives us such types, which he often draws, as the cruel father, or the selfish husband, or the stupid bully in 'The Man in a Case', 'The Head of the Family', 'The Husband', 'An Upheaval', 'At a Country House', 'Difficult People'. All this is implicit in Verotchka.

This simple manliness of the boy whose father had been a serf and with hard work bought himself free and kept a little store in Taganrog, down in the territory of the Don Cossacks, this hatred of nonsense, this desire for 'personal freedoms', gives us, secondly, the simplicity of Chekov's subjects. He is free of the Romanticism of the 1860s, as he is free of the Naturalism of the 1860s. 'He demanded from writers, ordinary topics from life, simplicity of narration and absence of effects or tricks. One has simply to write about how Peter got married to Marie.' (*Chekov.* Koteliansky, p. 20. London, 1927.) And in his sympathy with the people who had no nonsense about them, the common Russian people, we get many stories of great tenderness, or sometimes frank avowal, about the peasants. 'Easter Eve', a story of the Ukraine, is so tender in its moody fusion of self with the spirit of the dead canticle-writer, and the dark night and the ferry, and the gathering peasants that it has an unreserve of emotion rare in Chekov.

> I did not see (the dead) Nikolay. God knows, perhaps if I had seen him I should have lost the picture my imagination paints for me now. I imagine that lovable, poetical figure, solitary and not understood, who went out at nights to call to Ieronim over the water and filled his hymns with flowers, stars and sunbeams, as a pale, timid man with soft, mild, melancholy features.

The other side of the picture is in 'The Murder' or 'In the Ravine', or, 'The Witch'. He wrote of them with sympathy that never failed him: but he wrote of them without a shadow of sentimentality. 'There is peasant blood in my veins,' he said once, 'and you cannot astonish me with peasant virtues.' Gorki and Bunin, after him, it is said, alone spoke with the same directness about the peasant. There are no peasants in 'Verotchka': but there is the foil of that bourgeois stupidity and sentimentalism which made and kept them what they were.

Thirdly, and this is clear in 'Verotchka' and is one of the most important things to note in him:—'You may weep and moan over your stories, you may suffer together with your characters, but it should be done in such a way that the reader does not detect it. The more objective, the stronger the impression.' His reserve was immense: he might fuse himself with his people so that what he wrote they spoke; but at the same time—again, I say, it is an approach uniquely Chekovian—he would withdraw himself, as author, from participation in their self-belief. Not otherwise could he be truthful and at the same time natural. 'One ought to write only when one feels completely calm,' he said once, and that was what he doubtless meant by it. It is the mark of his ironic sympathy, as if a man smiled at the follies of his wife and still loved her for them. It is all part of his integrity as a man, which made him so hate sham, and like simple people, and yet not write of the shams without a twinkle or of the simple people without control over his affection.

Fourthly, and linked with this, is something which may have come to him by accident of his profession as a doctor, and partly, also, no doubt, from his admiration for Flaubert and Maupassant—the coldly objective, scientific eye of the student of physical diseases. It gives many of his stories a secondary interest which serves to buttress their emotional interest: an intellectual veracity, a content idea. You get something of a feeling that Doctor Chekov would have liked to cure these people of their neuroses, their extravagances, their insanity:

for he was loyal to his profession and acknowledged the help it gave him as an author.

I have no doubt that the study of medical sciences has had an important influence on my literary activity; they have considerably widened the range of my observations, and enriched me with knowledge, the true value of which to me as a writer, can be understood by one who is himself a doctor. They have also had a directing influence and it is probable that, thanks to my knowledge of medicine, I have managed to avoid many mistakes. My acquaintance with the natural sciences and with the scientific method has always kept me on my guard, and I have tried wherever possible to take the scientific data into consideration, and where this was impossible *I have preferred not to write at all.*

Similar emphases on the 'scientific method' are all over his letters. It helped him to keep his interest attached to the subject without engaging his emotions beyond what was proportionate to the cause.

So far I have listed:
1. Hatred of sham; but the keenest interest in it, as in everything.
2. Liking for simple subjects, simple people.
3. Reserve.
4. Scientific approach.

Now we must note something that enlivens and exalts all these things, a quality of his nature that became more and more personal to him as time went on, and which we might call the element of belief in him. He did sincerely believe in humanity. 'I am not a grave man, 'he said, and he could not understand why people called him a pessimist. Also—'From the days of my childhood I have believed in progress.' And his favourite phrase was: 'Look here, don't you see? There is sure to be a Constitution in Russia in ten years' time.' Kuprin records that, in Yalta, towards the end of his life,

> . . . he looked lovingly after his flower-beds, as if he saw in them the symbol of beauty to come, and watched new paths being laid out by human intellect and knowledge. He looked with pleasure at new and original buildings and at large, seagoing steamers: he was eagerly interested in every new invention and was not bored by the company of specialists. With firm conviction he said that crimes such as murder, theft, and adultery are decreasing, and have nearly disappeared among the intelligentsia—teachers, doctors and authors. He believed that in the future true culture would ennoble mankind.

His last work, *The Cherry Orchard*, expresses this eager, loving hope. 'How beautiful life will be in three or four hundred years!' Planting his garden he would joke about what he had done to change that one bit of wilderness. Then he would say, solemnly, 'Do you know that in three or four hundred years all the earth will become a flourishing garden?'

A man does not say such things unless he has grave need for optimism. You do not find optimists in palaces. I have prefaced this essay by one of his bitter condemnations of the Russia of his day, and he had, as a doctor, and as the investigator of Saghalien, the convict settlement, and as the poor boy of Taganrog, and as a man under sentence of death by consumption, grave need to believe in the future as an adjustment of the present. But he was no dreamer. He wanted to do things. How he scourges Souvorin in his letter of 9 March 1890, for saying that Saghalien is of no use to anyone, nor of any interest to anyone!

> It is evident from the books I have read and am reading that we have sent millions of people to rot in prisons, we have destroyed them at random, without reflection, barbarously: we have driven men through the cold in iron chains for thousands of miles: we have inflicted them with syphilis, depraved them, multiplied criminals, and for all this we have thrown the blame on the red-nosed prison superintendents. Now all Europe knows it is not the superintendents who are to blame, but all of us. But we do not care; it does not interest us. The glorified sixties did *nothing* for the sick and the prisoners and thus violated the chief commandment of Christian civilization.

Later he wants to go into the famine-stricken areas and work, and he goes about cadging money from his friends to help people.

How could he, then, as an artist fail to see that life posed questions, and that life had no answer for them? It is obligatory for an artist, he affirmed, to pose questions. As a man, a doctor, a friend in conversation he might try to answer these questions. But as an artist the sense of the inscrutable mystery of human suffering makes him stop when the problem has been stated. And so there thence comes into his work that sense of tears in human things which used to be foolishly taken for 'Russian Pessimism'.

> You scold me for my objectivity, calling it indifference to good and evil, lack of ideals and ideas and so on. When I describe horse thieves you would always have me say, 'Stealing horses is evil.' That was known long ago without me. Let the jury judge them. . . . I must tell you that they are not beggars but well-fed people, and that horse-stealing is not simple theft but a passion.

These, as I re-read him, strike me as the essential notes in the man's character. The note I find most important is the last, his faith in man. It is the element in him that induces me to think that had he not been a prose-writer he would have been a satirical poet.

2

Chekov began as a Naturalist. His models were Maupassant, Flaubert, Turgenev, Tolstoy. After Maupassant, indeed, he often felt that such demands had been imposed on the craft of the short-story that it was most difficult to work at all. His scientific approach, his insistence on conciseness, his truthfulness to fact, his clinical exactness when dealing with abnormalities or any physical phenomena, *his willingness to pose a problem and leave it at that*, his detachment—these are all in harmony with the ideals of naturalism. He is not a

Naturalist *pur sang*, however, and it is most interesting to note how he imposes on Naturalism his own personality, and yet how Naturalism crops up repeatedly and often spoils his stories, although it obviously helped him considerably to avoid the evils of sentimentality and cheap romanticism.

He touches whimsically on this when he describes to Souvorin the 'romantic' atmosphere of Suomy:

> Nature and life here are built on a pattern which has become old-fashioned now, and is discarded by editors. Not to speak of nightingales, which sing day and night, the barking of dogs heard in the distance, old neglected orchards, sad and poetical manor houses, nailed up and deserted, where live the souls of beautiful women. . . . Everything I see and hear now seems to be long familiar to me from old stories and tales. . . . There is a novelty of another kind. . . . On the eve of Whitsuntide all the maniacs will spend the night on the island and fish all night: I too. They are superb types.

And:

> A writer is a man bound, under contract, by the awareness of his duty and his conscience: taking the rope he must not say he can't pull: and whatever aversion he may feel he must overcome his fastidiousness, he must sully his imagination with the dirt of life.

There, if one left out Chekov's optimism, his thirst to believe, his sense of what was decent in life, his

106

pervasive kindliness, one might get the notion of another Maupassant. But though he admired these earlier writers as craftsmen, he had nothing in common with their pessimism. 'I wrote *Ivanov,*' he confessed, 'to summarize all that had been written about whining and gloomy people and to put an end to such writings.'

What distinguishes Naturalism from Chekovism is not matters of craft but *matters of faith.* Test this by characterization. He goes half-way with the Naturalists, or to put it correctly the Naturalists go half-way with him—as with everybody else before and after him, there being not five hundred ways of drawing a character, but only two or three, and Naturalism, or Realism, or Impressionism and so forth do no more than emphasize one of the two or three ways. For example, like the Naturalists, he is at pains to describe people by their outward appearance, but this is never done, except in his early or less satisfactory stories, for its own sake: which would be merely to give us a photograph of somebody who can be of no interest to us if we do not also know his inner nature. Take 'Mire', for instance—1888:

> The lieutenant sprang gaily out of his saddle, handed over his horse to a man who ran up, and stroking with his finger his delicate black moustache went in at the front door. On the top step of the old but light and softly carpeted staircase he was met by a maid-servant with a haughty, not very youthful face. . . . Exactly opposite the entrance, he saw sitting in a big, low chair, such as old men use, a woman in an expensive Chinese dressing-gown, with her head wrapped up, leaning back on a pillow. Nothing could be seen behind the woollen shawl in which she was muffled

but a pale, long, pointed, somewhat aquiline nose, and one large dark eye. Her ample dressing-gown concealed her figure, but judging from her beautiful hand, from her voice, her nose and her eye, she might be twenty-six or twenty-eight.

This is a photograph of any stranger in a photographer's show-case. It is not the real Chekov, and there is simply no point to it. Chekov did not work in this manner when at his best, and to return to our 'Verotchka' a year or two earlier, we see his more typical method there—still using externals, but with what different effect!

When Ognev later on remembered her, he could not picture pretty Verotchka except in a full blouse which was crumpled in deep folds at the belt and yet did not touch her waist: without her hair done up high and a curl that had come loose from it on her forehead: without the knitted red shawl with ball fringe at the edge which hung disconsolately on Vera's shoulders in the evenings, like a flag on a windless day, and in the day-time lay about, crushed up, in the hall near the men's hats or on a box in the dining-room, where the old cat did not hesitate to sleep on it. This shawl and the folds of her blouse suggested a freedom of feeling and laziness, of good-nature and sitting at home. Perhaps because Vera attracted Ognev he saw in every frill and button something naïve, cosy, something nice and poetical, just what is lacking in cold, insincere women that have no instinct for beauty.

There are two people's natures in that. This impressionistic method is his favourite one. So:

> Whenever I saw his neat spare figure, his high forehead and long mane of hair, when I listened to his speeches, *it always seemed to me . . .* etc. ('Excellent People.')

Or; wound into the narrative, speaking of a railway-manager:

> If you have asked him what his work was, he could look candidly and openly at you with his large bright eyes, through his gold pince-nez, and would answer in a soft velvety lisping baritone—'My work is literature.'

From 'The Lady with the Dog', the libertine's wife:

> She was a tall, erect woman with dark eyebrows, staid and dignified, and as she said of herself, intellectual. She read a great deal, used phonetic spelling, called her husband not Dmitri, but Dimitri, and he secretly considered her unintelligent, narrow, inelegant, was afraid of her, and did not like to be at home.

Externals are, in truth, of slight interest to Chekov, though he does not fail to value them in their place. For the minor character of the husband in 'The Lady with the Dog', he uses them well:

> He bent his head at every step and seemed to be continually bowing. Most likely this was the husband

109

whom at Yalta, in a rush of bitter feeling, she had called a flunkey. And there really was in his long figure, his side-whiskers, and the small bald patch on his head, something of the flunkey's obsequiousness: his smile was sugary, and in his buttonhole there was some badge of distinction like the number of a waiter.

There, two natures, the libertine's who watches, and the husband who is described, emerge from this impression. The complete objectivity of Maupassant's description of 'Boule de Suif' is rare in Chekov, and it is much more natural to him to say something like this:

Her expression was still childish and her figure was soft and slim: and her developed girlish bosom healthy and beautiful, was suggestive of Spring, real Spring.

An incident, a suggestive touch here and another little touch there, from the deeps of character—that is his method: and that these touches are carefully observed and selected one may easily see.

Now why do I say that what distinguishes this impressionistic, suggestive penetrative method from the objective externalizations of the Naturalists is less a matter of craft than of faith? Because he believes, in spite of everything, in men; their characters are to him an inner battlefield; it is to that personal battle that he wishes to penetrate. This is not the method of Zola, who does not believe in man, or indeed free-will at all; who sees man less as a man than as an animal, subject to powerful, irresponsible forces; who loves to make his battlefields out of the movements of great masses of men (as in *Germinal*) and not out of the struggles in individual creatures. Zola, as has often been remarked, is not interested in individuals, whom he is content to describe by *signes particuliers*, the label of a trick of voice, or a habit of speech, or a perpetual way of being silent and disdainful, like Souvarine in *Germinal*, or a perpetual way of always shouting like La Brûlé: beasts with no more than the infinitesimal distinctive marks of beasts. To Chekov there is in every man, even if he be a fool or a scoundrel, a sacred mystery to be plumbed. His 'touches' are like the entries of a doctor's notebook, recording each nature in the light of an implicit norm of health and sanity and decency. The artistic, giddy wife of the honest doctor in 'The Grasshopper'—a detail from life as Alexander Chekov tells us—will illustrate this. All Olga Ivanova's friends and acquaintances are at her wedding:

> 'Look at him; isn't it true that there is something in him?' she said to her friends with a nod towards her husband as though she wanted to explain why she was marrying a simple, very ordinary, and in no way remarkable man. . . . 'Now his face is turned three-quarters towards us in a bad light, but when he turns around look at his forehead. Ryabovsky, what do you say to that forehead? Dymov,' she called to her husband, 'hold out your honest hand to Ryabovsky.'

That 'honest hand' touch hits off the factitious quality of her nature to perfection. Later when the foolish grasshopper has an affair with Ryabovsky, she feels that he has painted some good pictures only because,

111

'thanks to her influence he had greatly changed for the better'. There we realize her conceit: and when her husband continues, in his kind way, to be gentle with her, and she says to Ryabovsky, and to everybody else who is aware of what is going on, 'That man crushes me with his magnanimity,' we know that she is a vain fool. When her husband falls ills with diphtheria she turns chill with horror, but what she says is, 'Why it's dangerous!' and we realize her-selfishness. Lastly when he is dying and she is filled with remorse, she only thinks:

> That silent, unrepining, uncomprehended creature, robbed by his mildness of all personality and will, weak from excessive kindness, had been suffering in obscurity somewhere on a sofa and had not complained. And if he were to complain even in delirium, the doctors watching by his bedside would learn that diphtheria was not the only cause of his sufferings. They would ask . . . etc.

It is a story whose touches give the typical Chekov, who is now the character he depicts, now the calm observer, now the doctor full of sympathy for his colleague whose life he has summed up in a few pages, but always *the moral judge.*

Of course he also relished odd detail for its own sake: that is the humourist in him. Such is the entry in his diary about the man who always spat at the University when he passed it, so that the cabby would pull up until he heard the spit go out behind them, and then—off again. Examples of these humorous details are the touch about the Lady with the Dog who 'was not sure whether her husband had a post in a Crown Department or under the Provincial Council—and was amused by her own ignorance'. Or when the Grasshopper's husband had to have his head shaved and she put a handkerchief around it and painted him as a Bedouin. Or the touch about the broken-down waiter in the fifth-class railway-bar who had once kept a buffet at a first-class station, and worn a dress suit and a gold chain: he now sells tea and vodka and sausages smelling of tar 'which he himself sarcastically said were only fit for the orchestra!' In the same story (The Murder'), Matvey writes into every book he borrowed from other people, considering it an obligation of politeness to do so, such inscriptions as:

> I, Matvey Terehov, have read this book and think it the very best of all the books I have read, for which I express my gratitude to the non-commissioned officer of the Police Department of Railways, Kuzna Nikolaev Zhukov, as the possessor of this priceless book.

Or there is the queer character in 'Rothschild's Fiddle' who keeps on thinking of his losses, due to the number of days on which he would not work, Sundays because it was a sin, Monday because it was unlucky, Saint's days, and so on.

> The thought of his losses haunted Yakov, especially at night: he laid his fiddle on the bed beside him and when all sorts of nonsensical ideas came into his head he touched a string. The fiddle gave out a sound in the darkness and he felt better.

He gets into such a melancholy condition after he has buried his 'old woman'—that too was a loss, for he himself made the coffin and would not be paid for it—that he imagines all the things he might have done, gone fishing and sold fish, played the fiddle from house to house, bred geese, 'Why the feathers alone would very likely mount up to ten roubles a year!' run boats—all losses, 'Ah, what losses, what losses!'

Yet, these too are touches that do not define but suggest, tease the heart and tickle the imagination until one becomes, in Chekov's hands, like Yakov's fiddle that gives out a sound in the darkness. One remembers them and one throbs again—the Privy Councillor who went to the country and said of everything, 'Come now, isn't that charming'; and he so upset everyone with ideas of his grandeur that the drivers took off their hats when they merely lifted down his trunks; and he was to have made the fortune of the little boy in the story, his nephew, and on the last day when he was actually bribed to go away he turned around and saw the child and cried out with a look of the utmost astonishment (he had seen the boy a hundred times), 'What little boy is this?'

No photographs, no absolute externality as of the Naturalists, then, for Chekov, and I find it the most admirable thing in him. He did say that he wished only to depict what he saw—but all writers say that, and he saw far more than most. Perhaps it is that he saw in his characters moments as well as men. That was the poet in him. He constantly wrought his people into situations that would satisfy this side of him, situations that opened little windows into their souls where they saw and confessed the mystery of a wider orbit of life than they or we commonly see, let alone admit, as we go about our daily trivialities.

114

3

To pass from people, his method of describing things and places affirms this difference between him and the Naturalistic writers whom he took as models. Here, too, he never ignores the value of external detail. He never over-estimates it. He will not be content, in one story, to say that a man hung his hat on a nail. He says, he hung his hat 'on a huge, misshapen nail'. But we note that the furniture of that man's house—it is Father Yakov, the poor priest of 'The Nightmare'—has been described with care just before, and that even this tiny detail of the nail is in some way proper to the character of the priest, and not there just for the sake of idle verisimilitude. We may note, too, that when he describes a snow-storm or a summer's day, it is fitted, by its tone-value or by its sub-audible comment on the action, into the story. Thus 'The Murder' opens with a religious service at a wayside station; he tells us that:

> all stood in silence, fascinated by the glare of the lights and the howling of the snow-storm which was aimlessly disporting itself outside, regardless of the fact that it was the Eve of the Annunciation.

We know that this is not simple picturesqueness; it impresses us with a sense of the mute suffering that holds these peasants in a kind of fatalistic effortlessness. The scene is part of them. The background of 'Easter Eve' creates, similarly, a sense of awe suitable to this story of the dead canticle-writer, mingled with joy for the feast and the resignation that falls benignly on the

115

narrator because of it. Note how un-photographic the description is, how near to poetry:

> The world was lighted by the stars, which were scattered thickly all over the sky. I don't ever remember seeing so many stars. Literally one could not have put a finger in between them. There were some as big as a goose's egg, others tiny as hempseed. . . . They had come out for the festival procession, every one of them, little and big, washed, renewed and joyful and every one of them was softly twinkling its beams. The sky was reflected in the water: the stars were bathing in its depths and trembling with the quivering eddies. The air was warm and still. Here and there, far away on the further bank in the impenetrable darkness, several bright red lights were gleaming . . .

The same suggestibility that we see in his personal descriptions occurs over and over in these descriptions of nature.

> When the service was over and the people going home it was warm and sunny: the water gurgled in the gutters, and the unceasing trilling of the larks, tender, telling of peace, rose from the fields outside the town. The trees were already awakening and smiling a welcome, while, above them, the infinite fathomless blue sky stretched into the distance, God knows whither.

Or, again—entirely impressionistic:

When the bishop got into his carriage to drive home, the gay melodious chime of the heavy, costly bells was

116

filling the whole garden in the moonlight. The white walls, the white crosses on the tombs, the white birch trees and black shadows, and the far away moon in the sky exactly over the convent, seemed now living their own life, apart and incomprehensible, yet very near to man.

It is all fused moodily into the heart of the story, welding Chekov and the Bishop who drives, and us who read, into a oneness that lasts as long as our memory of the story.

All the usual superfluous descriptions of the Naturalists he avoids. When the priest dictates and the deacon writes the letter, in the story called 'The Letter', is there a word about sitting down, getting paper or ink, scratching pen, 'the hand moving across the page' and so forth and so on? There is only this:

He made the deacon sit down to his table and began—'Write . . . Christ is risen . . .' (etc. to the end of the letter.) When he had finished writing the deacon read it aloud, beamed all over and jumped up.

Nor is there any of the Naturalist's brutality in Chekov—this again annotating what I have said about the nearness to poetry. A wealthy landowner is seen entering a poor church, which he is intended to hate and despise: and with all his natural tenderness and sympathy Chekov says only:

The wooden church was old and grey. The columns of the porch had once been painted white, but the colour had now peeled off and they looked like two

117

ungainly shafts. The ikon over the door looked like a dark, smudged blur. But its poverty touched and softened Kunin.

How Chekov must have worked, and cut, and cut, to fashion everything, like that small bit, into the unity of his mood. Or is it that he was really, instinctively a poet and with a poet's intuition could not conceive of an idea except as a perfect unity in all its parts?

4

One cannot write of Chekov without at least making mention of his irony—mention being all that is possible with so subtle an element of his nature and his work. It enters into his work from the beginning, but it does not deepen into full strength for many years—it is one sign of his constant growth.

His life falls, as the lives of so many men seem to do, into three parts, of which the middle part lies roughly between 1888 and 1898, contains a greater proportion of first-class work and is marked by a firmly-controlled ironic humour.

After he had matriculated from the grammar-school at Taganrog in 1879 he had gone to Moscow where he lived with his people in such poverty that he wrote comic stories as much from necessity as desire. These were collected in *Stories of Melpomena* (1884) and *Motley Stores* (1885). He had regarded them 'lightly, carelessly, casually'—so he said—and could not remember a story that took longer than a day to write. (Later on he was to keep stories by him for more than a year.) This kind of thing he was still writing in 1885 when he was a doctor, and a few lines of one will show the level of his work, and suggest, too, that Gorki is right in saying that a great deal of cruelty and disgust lie hidden behind the humorous words and phrases, observed and concealed. He calls this squib 'Life is Wonderful':

Life is quite an unpleasant business but it is not so very hard to make it wonderful. . . . When your matches suddenly go off in your pocket rejoice and offer thanks to heaven that your pocket is not a gunpowder magazine. When your relations come to pay you a visit during your holiday in the country, don't get pale but exclaim triumphantly, How very lucky it's not the police. . . . Rejoice that you are not a tram-horse, nor a Koch bacillus, nor a trichina, nor a pig, nor an ass, nor a bear led by a gipsy, nor a bug. . . . If you are flogged with a birch rod, kick your legs in rapture and exclaim, How very happy I am that I am not being flogged by nettles. If your wife has been unfaithful to you, rejoice that she has betrayed merely yourself and not your country.

Indeed it is hardly humorous. It is the kind of bitter thing a thousand poor hacks turn out daily for our newspapers, except that they dare not go even so near the bone of satire. Yet he was sufficiently merry and content during those years and was too hard at work on his medical studies to have time to collect himself, to ponder quietly. Grigorovitch's letter of encouragement came after he had managed to get out of the funny papers into the *Petersburg Gazette* and, from that on, he worked for Souvorin and other reputable editors; the volume of 1887, *At Twilight*, marking his first output of serious work, and the tone of his letters from 1886 onward marking a new note of self-confidence. He was by this date working as Medical Attendant at the Zemstvo Hospital of Zvenigorod, some fifty miles from Moscow. But he had, already in 1884, seen in himself the first signs of consumption, and in April 1886 had a second and more serious haemorrhage. In 'The Steppe', to probe no deeper—it was the result of a journey in South Russia in 1887—we find a note of deeper irony and melancholy that, taken with, say 'The Nightmare' (1887), may be said to mark the end of his first period.

By 1890 the iron has entered his blood. In that year he makes his journey across Siberia to examine conditions in the convict settlement of Saghalien, and his letters, I have quoted a few lines of one, reveal how much he has begun to ponder on the harder and more cruel side of life in Russia. Plescheyev had about this time spoken of a 'tendency' in his work; at the end of 1889 he already writes:

> You once told me that my stories lack the protesting element, that there are no sympathies and antipathies in them. But in this story ('A Tedious Story') do I not from beginning to end protest against falsehood? Is not that a tendency? No? Well, then, I cannot bite, or I am a flea.

He protests, 'comments' I would say, a good deal in this period in 'The Duel', 'The Grasshopper', 'The Wife', 'Neighbours', and bitterly, I think, over-naturalistically, in such stories as 'The Chorus Girl', all between 1891 and 1894. The peasant stories, such as 'Murder' (1895) are a terrible comment on the Russia he was now seeing, while 'The Black Monk' (1894) and 'My Life' (1896) comment on the banality of the bourgeois life of the provinces. Meanwhile he is never free of illness and is being constantly ordered by the doctors to the Crimea or the South of France.

His letters of these years are often serious, 'protesting', analysing, troubled, concerned with current ideas, and must be taken with his medical and humanitarian work from 1892 on when he buys a farm at Melikhovo some seventy-five miles south of Moscow, fights cholera, or builds schools, mostly out of his own pocket. Thought and work are here of a piece, as when (1889) he curses the French and lashes the Russian intelligentsia and praises the Germans—our 'drowsy, apathetic, lazily philosophizing, cold intelligentsia'; 'Germany knows nothing of authors like Bourget and Tolstoy and in that she is lucky: in Germany there is science, love of country, diplomatists . . . She will beat France, and her allies will be French authors.' This interest in ideas, this attitude to life in his private work, sturdy active and even hopeful, mingled with frequent depressions; 'We writers have neither immediate nor remote aims, and in our souls a great emptiness' (1892); or sudden enthusiasms, as for Zola in the Dreyfus affair, are reflected in his stories, which like 'A Man in a Case', Ionitch', or 'The Lady with the Dog' are now never free of an ironic mood. An instinctive artist, he did in this period from, say, 1888 to 1898, both his best work and his worst. Wherever pity fails and cruelty enters, a quality alien to him, one may guess at a low period of health and spirits. He was so much a man who wrote out of his whole self that there is nothing in him of the even-ness of the 'pure artist' like Flaubert or Turgenev. Irony was his one defence against despair. Without it he tended to write out of an abstract disgust. With it he could retain pity and love. A born humorist, too, he always had to laugh at something—smile wanly might be a better word—even if only at himself.

He emigrated to Yalta, his 'warm Siberia', in 1899, and was married in 1901. Of this third period it is not in his stories but in the melancholy tenderness of *The Three Sisters* and *The Cherry Orchard* that we find the true expression of the man; and if one does not see in these plays a constant groan of, now, almost weary irony one will see nothing but atmosphere. He wrote *The Cherry Orchard* in 1903, planned it in January, began it about July, and had it finished by September. He died in Badenweiler on 2 July 1904.

He had lived a comparatively lonely and private life, and even after his marriage he lived alone, his wife more often living in Moscow than with him. 'It is so dull here,' he said to Bunin, in Yalta. 'The only excitement is when the telephone rings and Sophie Pavlovna asks what I am doing and I answer "I am catching mice".' (Which, by the way, when he had caught he would take to the end of the garden and release again.) He wrote, 'As I shall lie alone in the grave so, indeed, do I live alone.' A thoughtful, serious, merry-hearted, sensitive man, always brooding, always smiling ironically over the result of his thoughts.

5

There is one thing about him that will specially interest Irish writers. He was Russian in his work, but he was never regionalist in his thought. You may find in his work traces of his life in Taganrog, in Melikhovo, in Saghalien, in the Ukraine—a writer does not invent life!—but the things that were the foundation of his attitude to life, his gospel of normality, was wide as the world: he never concerned himself as an artist with such things as Slavophilism, or with any other kind of 'movement'. He detested movements. 'Labels' or 'prejudices' were his words for any kind of 'warfare' in literature. He concerned himself only with decency, lies, the frustration of the individual soul, personal freedom, sham, cant, human folly and human virtue in all its oldest forms: he believed in Christianity, much as Balzac did, and made it the framework of his personal idea of what life should be like, though he had no definite creed and did not believe in personal immortality. He had only one conscious aim, to depict life faithfully so as to show how it departed from *the norm*.

As to what the norm was, it was certainly not any specifically Russian idea of normality. 'I do not know, and you do not know,' he said, 'what the norm is.' 'We all know what a decent act is but what honour is we do not know. I shall keep to the framework nearest my heart, which has already been tried by men stronger, and wiser than I. The framework is the absolute freedom of man, freedom from violence, from prejudices, ignorance, the devil, one's passions, etc.' The result was that his stories are valid wherever they are read.

123

They have none of the merely peculiar or picturesque interest of the regionalist writer whose characters live as he himself lives by a local norm. Their validity is not abstract or doctrinal, such as is asked for by social and religious regionalists. Chekov was a man who was content to know little, in an abstract way, about life and its meaning. He was content to put down what he saw, truthfully, kindly and without rancour, as an honourable and decent-minded man-of-the-world—a Russian man-of-the-world, no doubt, steeped in Orthodoxy—and let his readers draw from his work what conclusions they could or would, each according to his power and deserts. As such he wrote the universe into Russia.

The source of Chekov's attraction is not hard to see. It is his personal quality of mind—his sanity in the face of a chaos of moral and social values no less perplexing then than now. He had the personal integrity and wit to see that the French writers of the 1830s onward, and their Russian offshoots like Lermontov and Tyutchev, were fine craftsmen but had no adequate 'gospel of normality'. He rejected them because he was integrated as they never were. He broke down in his work the wall that they erected between art and life, and if he did not as Balzac said of his own work, 'make Society wear upon its brow the reasons of its being' he did demand from life in Russia what Balzac, also, called 'an inward meaning'. His work was, in its effect, a constructive criticism of life. The foundations of that criticism, its standards of reference, were with him, as with Balzac, Christian foundations. It is true that neither of them, as far as one can see, gave to a supernatural Christianity their utter and absolute belief, but they did believe in the Christian 'system' and gave it their loyalty with heart and admiration, and based on it all they had to say or think about human behaviour. It is this thirst for normality that, to my mind, gives his firmness to Chekov. He never forces it. It need hardly be said that he never preaches. At most one is aware of his ironically critical eye. But the implications are always there—even in so apparently slight and gossamer a tale as 'Verotchka'. It means that his stories, are always vertebrate.

6

For the purposes of this book one other question poses itself. Was Chekov fundamentally a 'romantic' or a 'realist'? A reader who may think of his tales and plays in such terms as charming, evocative, atmospheric, poetic, even picturesque, may also easily find himself thinking of them as romantic. And yet, if Chekov is a moral writer, as I think he insistently is in the sense that Balzac was a moral writer, how can one use such an adjective about the one without using it about the other? And nobody would wish to call Balzac a romantic except as a challenge to finer definitions as Faguet does when he calls Zola 'a debauched romantic'.

Both Balzac and Chekov are realists in the sense that for both there is an established norm of decent human nature and behaviour, a standard and a touchstone, solid, permanent and widely accepted, their common earth on which their characters stand or fall, and which is their notion of reality. They are gregarious men, men in society, men with social consciences and an historical sense and such men need permanent references and checks. The romantic not only does not need these controls but dislikes them because they tie him down, compel him to make comparisons and come to conclusions when he would prefer to let his subject expand and vanish as rhetoric or gesture, exhaust itself orgiastically or evaporate into mood or poetic feeling, as so often happens, and so delightfully, with Daudet.

This sense of space is denied to the realist; its delights and freedoms and illusions are not for him; he finds his recompense in Time, in the past, present and future, in that shadow which guarantees to everybody with a historical sense the pleasure and pain of memory, intense interest in the present, some hope and frequent despairs for the future. This time-sense gives to the realist sorrows and visions so intensely felt that your extremist in realism—among whom we must count Maupassant—will easily become a misanthrope or a madman. For Time cheats. It takes away more than it gives. A too-great awareness of it always induces unhappiness, and the happiest people are those with no sense at all of time. This is why realists are always more likely to be gloomy than cheerful, and why romantics are not so much gloomy as melancholy—for the autumn, before a dying fire, at twilight, thinking of love elsewhere, or of an imaginary better life elsewhere. 'Fade far away, dissolve and quite forget': the romantic Keats. 'How beautiful life will be in three or four hundred years': the realist Chekov.[1] It is this realist hope, or sense, of development, sense of history, of change,

---

[1] My idea that the romantic has no time-sense might seem to be contradicted by his notorious love of the past. But it is a dream-past, never an historical past. Compare, for example, the Pre-Raphaelites' idealization of the Middle Ages with an historian's picture.

of man in action which demands of the realist an objectivity which is of secondary interest to the romantic. Today when we are all, to some degree or other, realists, we find critics unconsciously proving the truth of this by their way of picking out from the romantics, like Tennyson, the more objective runs, and so praising them for being such good romantic poets on the head of far from characteristically romantic achievements. I must add that I am here consciously avoiding the same pitfall. I am suggesting no *critical* comparisons between realist and romantic. They are merely different temperaments, attitudes, needs, gifts and names. Indeed the whole burthen of these first two essays on Daudet and Chekov is that the first unwisely forced his temperament out of its mould, borrowed attitudes, imagined needs he did not have, and that Chekov wisely kept to his gamut. Chekov did not write novels, and when he wrote plays he invented a special technique for his special temperament. All one can say is that he was, as a writer, evidently much more adult and intelligent than Daudet.

It is evident, equally, that he was a realist of his own special sort and not of anybody else's sort. He held on to poetry, to mood, to poetic feeling. He found an original way of doing this and at the same time of being true to common life. There are no characters in Chekov whom Flaubert might not have written about; no situations that are abnormal, there is no psychology which the average man in the street could not recognize. Indeed what puzzles most ordinary readers coming on him for the first time is not that his subjects and people are unusual but that they are, apparently, banal. 'They just wander around the stage talking!' Conversely what sometimes deludes the sophisticated is the poetry in which he seems to drown this banality, so that they see the beautiful mists and fail to see behind these mists the hard, mocking mind of the doctor, the moralist and the judge. Both simple and sophisticated thus lose contact with the author's personality. It is not that he is over-subtle. It is, simply, that he is a doctor who writes his diagnoses as poetry, so that he sometimes reminds me of Italian primitives at whose work one looks in such delight that not for a long time does one perceive that it is as lifelike as it is lovely. This balance is, to me, what he meant by saying that a writer needs maturity and a sense of personal freedom: it is his way of saying, I suggest, that a writer must be a civilized man. As for what he meant by that—it is his own nature projected in his stories.

4

GUY DE MAUPASSANT
OR *THE RELENTLESS REALIST*

Any young man who may think that the best short-stories are written by the best technicians would do well
to get hold of Emile Faguet's *Propos Littéraires* and read
the essay, in the third volume, on Maupassant.

To Faguet, in this essay, Maupassant was simply a
man who took the banana of life and ate it. 'His mind
was a sort of mechanical cutter' (what printers and
tailors would, I suppose, call a guillotine—when they
do not, in Dublin at any rate, call it a *gullotin*) 'which
he levelled consistently on the confused flux and flow
of things.' His mind, that is, chopped off such bits of
reality as had a certain unity or central point capable
of being worked up into a story or a novel. He had
no theories, no doctrines, no technical method such
as Zola had, for example. He was the least *livresque* of
writers. All his friends agree on this. At a dinner-table
he would enjoy talking about the water-cure but hate
talking about octavos. He almost disliked books. He
never even tried to observe life. That is, he was not a
deliberate and scientific observer. 'He knew that if you
accost reality you cannot help deforming it by the very
impact of your ambush.' Meaning that we can provoke
life into making the sort of answers that we would like
it to make, much as we can do with a man by putting

him through, a third-degree. Life, in short, fell into Maupassant's mould and came out as stories. That is all there was to it, concludes M. Faguet, smiling blandly.

And so, his books, without telling us anything about his life, follow the course of his life. He is a Norman: ergo, stories about Normans—Norman peasants, Norman squireens, Norman fishermen, Norman publicans. He was twenty in 1870; ergo, stories about the war in Normandy, and always in so far as he actually saw it himself, with the middle-classes terrified and the peasants playing possum cunningly and craftily, and here and there in some passionate soul a sudden outburst of accumulated hate or of anger too long restrained. He next becomes a Parisian and mingles with the literary and journalistic world: the result, *Bel-Ami*. He is employed for some time in the Ministry—*L'Héritage*. He goes hiking in the mountains—*Mont Oriol*. In Italy—*Les Sœurs Rondoli*. Towards the end of his all too-short life he enters the worldly world, and then we get artists and *femmes du monde*—*Fort Comme la Mort, Notre Cœur*. He penetrates the demi-monde—*Yvette*.

I have a profound respect for the critical faculties of Emile Faguet but this does not impress me. (Which does not mean that it ought not to impress the young man I have imagined; no young man has the right to be unimpressed by his elders.) We others do no more titan say, 'And so. Daudet went hiking in the hills and out came *Mont Oriol*, and, Maupassant went hiking in the hills and out came *Tartarin de Tarascon*.' For all that, what Faguet has done is only to overstate a sound point. It is true that Maupassant's realism is so real that we might well think we find in his books neither a man, nor a style, nor an author—only people and things. Nothing has flawed that translucent mirror in which we see those things. The mirror does not exist. Maupassant does not exist. It is a most forcible way of saying that his realism is the peak of its kind.

It is also nonsense. No writer can put down just what he sees if to say so carries the implication that he has chosen not to see other things. As we shall notice later what Maupassant leaves out is as much as what Maupassant puts in. Not that this affects his merits since it is equally true of every writer in the world, barring only the three or four giants who must not be introduced into any form of literary criticism since they are above and beyond it; which means that he is, therefore, at least as inclusive as any other writer, and that the only opinion we are entitled to utter on this count is that he is not among those very few whom we call the Great; and this we might know without having to think about it. Likewise it does not matter to his merits if we conclude, therefore, that he does undoubtedly select what he chooses to see. But it does obviously, and literally, mean that he has, contrary to M. Faguet's opinion, a *manière de voir.*

What has led Faguet to adopt so extreme an attitude is three-fold. (i) He is what he himself calls a Pantagruelist, that is, a man who takes things as they are and does not keep on hoping they will presently become something else; a man who so loves life that he does not need to hope for a better; a man who has therefore a consistent *mépris des fortuits*, who never takes a ticket in the Lottery; and who, as for religion,

131

will at most, if hard-driven, raise his eyes to the majestic consolation of another life better even than this excellent one. (2) This leads him, in this essay at any rate, dangerously near to what I call the Divine Plumber theory of literature, which is first cousin to the God's-in-His-Heaven theory, and the All-for-the-best-in-the-best-possible world theory. In this theory the gods attend to every writer's spiritual fountain—supply the pipes, the source, the jet, the necessary compression, and even the sun to sparkle on the spray, and if a goldfish gets stuck in the pipes . . . why, the gods will attend to him too. In other words, a writer is just a fellow who writes. (3) Lastly, what has drawn Fauguet into this extreme position is that he not only agrees with all Maupassant's judgments but cannot see how Maupassant could possibly have formed any other judgment, since to do so would be to disagree with M. Faguet. For this is what he, too, would have judged, would have selected, would have *seen*, i.e. decided to see, if he had been a writer.

Without thinking of it he has, in the process (of painting the middle order of human nature), drawn up certain statistics. They are pretty well exact. The number of egoists, passionate men, imbeciles and misfits that he has indicated seems just about right. . . . The middle order of human beings really are more or less like that: very few real sinners, a great many weak souls, an infinite number of egoists, that is Maupassant's world, and it agrees roughly with my own estimate. The impartial tranquillity of his observation has produced results which are not far from absolute exactitude.

132

Put any normal man (i.e. a Maupassant or a Faguet) on this job and this is what he must chop out of the 'confused flux and flow' of things. In other words Maupassant is the perfect Pantagruelist. Should all literature, then, and all life, be tested by Maupassant's 'statistics'? One turns the pages hastily to see what M. Faguet thinks about, say, Eugénie de Guérin or Barbey d'Aurevilly. The reading is pleasant, because he is so kind and sympathetic—as pleasant as his own essay 'Sur le Mensonge'. As one would expect of so civilized a man he approves of lies to pretty ladies, to the sick, and in poetry, which is to make the circuit of realism, back to Maupassant, the man who never told a lie, who never flattered, whose incorruptible, unassuageable, unalterable low opinion of mankind is what the happy Stoic naturally loves to hear and to believe since it absolves him from the least urge towards hope. Not that Faguet is a pessimist but that he knews that only optimists are sad men—for them it will always be jam tomorrow.

At this point the young man who wants to learn about 'technique' will be completely at his ease. He will observe that there is a point of view in the writer, and a point of view in the critic, and a point of view in the critic's critic, and he must presume that a point of view is expected of him, too, towards all three, and towards everything else as well. He will be at his ease because it is precisely this which puts every writer at his ease, liberating him from all compulsions by inviting him to surrender to himself. For the theory of the impersonal writer, he will begin to perceive, is an illusion, and no story-writer so fully betrays himself (i.e. surrenders to himself), in practice, as the man who cultivates complete impersonality. It is no trouble to any critic to write an essay on the personal views of Flaubert; the sangfroid of Stendhal does not conceal the man; the silences (i.e. the omissions) of Maupassant are eloquent of his personal views of life.

<h2 style="text-align:center">2</h2>

Here our young man meets the inevitable two schools of thought. They are, in this case, the romantic and the realist; for whether Maupassant is or is not a realist in any historical meaning of the word, he is definitely an anti-romantic; and so is Faguet. Our young man cannot avoid partiality; the question poses itself inexorably. If he loves Daudet's stories, if he loves Chekov beyond all other writers of the *nouvelle*, he must do so either because he thinks of Daudet and Chekov as romantics or because he thinks of them as realists. If he likes or if he detests Zola it must be for the same reason that induced him to like or detest Chekov. At an earlier period there was a sort of split-alternative—one could say that Balzac or Flaubert were half-romantic, or that Stendhal was half-realist. By Maupassant's day it is a case of 'Under which flag?'

The question is not simple. As an approach to the 'realism' of Maupassant it is informative to reassess the 'realism' of Zola. Zola imposed himself on the world as a realist; he is, like Daudet in his novels, bubbled with romanticism. All his contemporaries suspected this; every critic has since accepted it that Romance was his father and his mother and his *bête-noir*; he feared it himself and was sensitive to any criticism that suggested it. The result was that those who wished to praise his temperament and his work without adverting to the overblown character of both said that he wrote epics; those who wished to advert to his romantic quality and yet to flatter him said that he was a poet; those who wished, gently, to define his temperament and his work proposed to him that he had a lyrical nature which tended a little (?) to exaggerate the truth. Confident that he was relying on documents and facts, and on his reason rather than his imagination, Zola felt that he was unassailably a realist and did not therefore mind being called a poet. (Who would?) He had his own formula to defend his exaggerations.

> I exaggerate. That is quite true. But I do not exaggerate as did Balzac, just as Balzac did not exaggerate as did Victor Hugo. The whole point is there: the work proceeds from the conditions of the operation. We all of us tell some lies, but the question is what is the mechanism and what is the quality of the lie? Now I believe that I lie in the direction of truth. I am afflicted with a hypertrophia of whatever is true in point of detail, rising starwards from the springboard of observation. For reality soars upward with a stroke of the wing towards the symbol . . .

He could say this without realizing that it is a form of definition of the romantic flight.

We may leave it to Faguet to list the marks of the 'romantic' in the 'realist'. He saw big, a sort of mirage between him and fact that so swelled it that every hillock became a mountain. Things with him were more alive than men. This delicate and brooding sense of the mysterious life of the inanimate universe had been

135

one of the greatest inventions of the original romantic spirit. With him what happens? Shops, mines, locomotives are living villains and heroes in his tales. With him, as with all romantics, descriptions spill over—become ponds, lakes, very oceans of picture-making. In him the romantic melancholy had its apogee. He says he uses his reason, but what depth or edge has this reason of his? He loathes finesse; wit is beneath him; an agile thought, a penetrating observation, an epigram are, to a prodigious degree, beyond his ken. He alleged that he used *only* his reason; in fact he swam in his imagination like a fish; for he did not really like truth-to-life at all, being in that like all romantics who feel that it limits them, represses their flights, chokes their eloquence. And all this goes side by side with the most painstaking documentation, creeps into its interstices, crumbles it, and topples it, so that while the details, as he calls them, are almost all concrete and correct (he made slips of fact here and there, but that is no matter) the characters are never concrete human beings; they are abstractions recognizable and distinguishable only by his awful trick of giving to each a single posture, even no more than a *tic* (a device which Daudet also practised in his novels), but never those nuances, complexities or contradictions which an elementary psychology discovers in all men. Zola had another formula for this technique of 'the abstraction of the personage' as he called it. Defending its use in *Germinal* against Henri Ceard, he said:

> My novel is a great fresco in which each major character had to be foreshortened, and minor characters sketched by a line. But each has his own proper movement, as for instance Etienne, whose mind

fills gradually with Socialist ideas. I do not therefore understand your regret that I did not create individuals instead of limiting myself to a picture of the crowd. My subject was the action and reaction of the crowd and individual. How could I then have produced this effect if I did not, as you allege, create individuals?

Patently the man does not know what an individual person is: how could he, inside the deterministic philosophy which was the basis of his literary creed?

What he is, cries Faguet, is a debauched romantic. He is what romanticism becomes in the hands of any uncultivated man who is ignorant of the classics and of foreign literature, its picturesque quality debased into blaring colour and loud noise, so that, as painters say, it makes things scream instead of making them sing; its wealth of feeling and its variety of sensations reduced to the poverty-stricken and brutal simplicity of a formula in which man is less than a brute; its despairing sorrow coarsened into a general hatred of society, and indeed human nature, all being exactly what the equally uncultivated reader entirely approves because it drags him along, forcibly, without effort on his part, by its vehemence, exaggeration and continual hyperbole. Tchaikowsky's D flat and the bawling of the last Act in *La Boheme*.[1]

[1] As everybody knows, Zola was never approved by the élite of French criticism—e.g. Brunetière, Lemaître or Anatole France. The French Academy rejected his application thirty-seven times. The judgment of Anatole France was savage: 'His work is bad. He is one of those unfortunates whom one may say that it would have been better had he never been born. I do not, to be sure, deny him his detestable glory. No man ever so clearly disowned, as far as

To turn from this *poete barbare* to Maupassant might not at first glance seem to be to turn to a very resounding contrast on any count, especially if our first impression of Maupassant should be gathered from that type of anthology with which British and American publishers have tended to exploit his popular reputation for salacity. But if he be read in French and in bulk, the two first requisites for the full appreciation of his genius; and if, further, his achievement be related to the conventions of French life and literature, his distinct position will gradually assert itself. His realism is cleansed of all romantic impurities.

He is the most uncompromising of all the French realists: he presents, that is to say, the more bitter element in French literature and French character with a devastatingly quiet assumption that no other way of regarding life is possible. He does not preach or moralize, or praise, or condemn: he simply presents. His main quality is persuasiveness combined with chilliness. He is so cold that even if we feel that he is being hateful we cannot be angry; we can only laugh uncomfortably without even the comfort of feeling that he responds with a smile, since, if that stolid Norman face ever does smile, it is with the famous *sourire caché* of his great teacher Flaubert. Compared to his immobile features the 'Mona Lisa' grins from ear

---

that is concerned, all humanity's ideals.' Faguet does not deny him qualities, such as his marvellous power in painting crowds, some splendid openings and moving climaxes. 'Un poète barbare, un Hugo vulgaire et brut, mais puissant, un démiurge gauche, mais robuste. . . une sorte de démon étrange qui tenait le milieu entre Promethée et Caliban. 'This does not mean that Anatole France could not admire Zola as a man; e.g. in the Dreyfus Affair.

to ear. Nor has this misanthropic sangfroid any of the modern American's swagger of toughness. Somebody has called him a *Huron de génie*. Our American friends, familiar with the wooden Indian figures outside their old tobaccoshops, will appreciate the image. In any case the toughness of American toughs is only skin-deep. It is a purely physical brutality. They are never half so brutal about the sentiments as they are about the senses, whereas he is ruthless straight through to the heart. Their toughness is never the result of a decision about life; it is partly a reflection of the surface of their own lives, partly a technique of dealing with life, never an opinion about it—they burk at drawing the logical conclusion of their own behaviour; whereas the brutality of the French is a judgment, all inclusive. The readiest illustration of this is to compare the sentimental treatment of women in American fiction with the equality of the sexes as demonstrated in Maupassant's impartially low opinion of both. It is touching that the American realists should show themselves chivalrous romantics immediately a little powdered snout appears among the gorilla backs and the hairy chests, but it is not logical and it makes one very suspicious of the totality of their work.

With this coolness goes something in Maupassant which readers of English literature take some time to appreciate, for it is more in accord with the French way of looking at things than our way. He made upon French readers the impression of being, in every sense of the word, one of their most healthy writers. Zola may have been partly responsible for his contemporary reputation in this regard, for he first described to the public Maupassant's vigorous way of life—his love of physical exercise, of the open-air, his high spirits, his fondness for boating and hunting. A French Hemingway?

'We all' says Lemaître, 'began talking about his *santé*, in fact it became his mark in popular opinion and nobody was more often proclaimed sound and sane than this young man who was to die unsound and insane.'

In any case something of the young 'Huron' emerges from his books themselves: his evident sympathy for strong masculine peasant types, such as old Hautot in that excellent story 'Hautot père et fils'; the satisfaction with which he describes physical sounds, colours, smells—'Une Idylle', 'Les Sœurs Rondoli'; the sense of oneness between man and nature, especially in regard to the passions; see those strangely affecting passages of natural description which lighten the savagery of *L'Héritage*; add the fact that he skipped the reflective side of man, as Henry James has pointed out, or at any rate reflection as addressed to anything higher than the gratification of an instinct, and that, even so, he addresses himself to the most elementary instincts—for instance, Norman avarice, as in 'Le Diable'; and that his line was as hard and clear as a diamond on glass; add that in all he did one feels his own enormous pride and self-assurance. All this builds up a general impression of clean, muscular force. Beside him Flaubert smells of the study; and there is a mustiness as of accumulated note-books about Zola; both seem (as indeed they are) paunchy and preserved. As for any suggestion that this writer was a subjective, or introspective or dreamy romantic soul—what mainly emerges is what Henry

James called 'the hardness of form, the hardness of nature'.

Add, next, his rude, even crude, health in the moral sense; that which so pleased the Pantagruelist in Faguet; which made Lemaître distinguish between sensuality, which he recognizes in Maupassant as a form of faunlike ignorance of good and evil, and obscenity, or *grivoiserie*, which is, of its offensive nature, in Europe, a Christian characteristic—that is, it offends and implies offence, and so is at least a back-handed acknowledgment of what it offends. Of this leering obscenity we find no trace in Maupassant. This quality Henry James also recognized while insisting that the innocence of the faun involves much savagery and more ignorance. (These are not his words but they are his meaning.) Arthur Symons went so far as to find him a writer in whom we always find a moral idea, though not necessarily the moral idea we might approve, contrasting him with Kipling, in whom he can find no moral idea. Wrong, crass, savage, simpliste in his view of life; absurd, mad with arrogance—we may feel him one or all of these things, but we cannot feel that he is evil or touched by evil since this is a term that simply does not enter into his vocabulary. On the contrary, in this man's writings, whose life was certainly far from chaste and pure, we feel the sheerness and coldness of early morning light—of March, or perhaps November—for one cannot suggest that there is anything in him even so near the sunny season as to be autumnal or of the spring. There are no suggestive half-lights in Maupassant. We see the prostitute, the beastly peasant, the timid bourgeois, the civil servant—his favourite subjects—in an unpitying light that exposes their wrinkled faces, their painted gums, their frayed cuffs, their shifty eyes, their hearts that have dried like peas. There is in his tales nothing of the diaphanous prurience of de Kock, the wet lips of Zola, the sense of sin that is all over Mauriac. Indeed there is in much of Maupassant the healthy disgust and contempt of what somebody has called a Pagan puritan.

But in many other ways he is the most ascetic of writers—no prolonged descriptions, no indulgence in 'atmosphere', no elaborate psychology, the simplest of subjects, the most unexceptional characters, a classical discipline of the imagination that not so much prunes as excludes all irrelevancies, and rigidly subordinates everything to the indicated aim, as complete an effacement of self as seems possible this side of a *procès-verbal*, and a style as laconic as a judgment from the bench. He touched the uttermost boundaries of classical realism. Anybody who persisted beyond him could only do what Zola did, round the world and find himself back in the romantic morass.

3

How much does one pay for this? For in literature one always pays. A writer chooses his gamut and, having chosen, cannot go outside it, as Daudet proved to his cost. Let us take three examples of Maupassant's work to observe his gain and loss. I choose, first, a story in which we can the more easily, though for that reason somewhat unfairly, observe the loss.

'Une Soirée' is a story in which a cavalry-sergeant, suddenly hard-up, decides to visit, after many years, a married sister living in a country town in Brittany. Now this is one of the oldest romantic subjects in the history of the short-story. Twenty Years After is as appealing a theme as Snow at Christmas or The Return of the Prodigal. 'Une Soirée', however, illustrates Maupassant's way of treating all romantic situations in a realistic way. To start, the sergeant's motive is such as a gentler writer like Chekov (a) would never have considered sufficient and (b) would never have revealed bluntly at the beginning.

> It was not that he loved Mme. Padoie, who was a little pious creature much given to moralizing and always in a state of nerves; he needed money, badly, and he had just remembered that of all his relatives the Padoies were the only ones he had never touched.

There is the clean hard line without an iota of indulgence. And if one should say, 'But surely Sergeant Varajou must have felt some little sentimental feeling?' one will merely run full tilt against Maupassant's uncompromising 'morality', and his habit of deliberately choosing extrovert characters whose nature does not contain any such nuances. If the romantic or the humanist further insists that even the simplest natures possess these nuances—and if Chekov is one's love one will call him to bear witness to this—Maupassant will seem to look at us with his heavy-lidded eyes and give an all but imperceptible shrug. That may be our view of life: it is not his.

'So, Varajou, alighting from the train, drives to his brother-in-law's house.' No waste of words there. Old Padoie is in his office, he looks up and says, 'Wait'. Not

143

a very romantic reunion. Varajou looks at him, as he waits, and says to himself, 'What a moron!' Straight and plain. Can we say too straight and plain? But:

> This man was one of those brawling noisy fellows for whom life has no pleasures more refined than the pub and the prostitute. Beyond those two poles of existence he understood nothing. A boaster and a blatherer, full of contempt for everybody, he despised the entire universe from the pinnacles of his ignorance. Once he had said, 'Good Lord, what fun I'm having!' he had climbed the highest peak of admiration of which he was physically capable.

He meets his sister. At once she tells him the fine things she's heard about his goings on, and that is that. He goes off with a flea in his ear, to wander around the utterly dull and sleepy town, groaning, 'Lord, this is going to be a trial', and returns for supper in the damp dining-room 'with the paper peeling near the wainscot'. When he foresees an evening alone with his sour-spirited sister, for the husband has to go out to M. the Minister—the Padoies are recognized as most respectable and religious folk and move in the highest 'society' of Vannes—he makes some excuse to escape for the night, seeks out the biggest café, and sits to his coffee and brandy. The dull plonk of billiard-balls is the only sound in the café, except when five or six clients come in to chat, in low voices, elbows on tabletops. The sergeant has another bottle of brandy. Soon he wants to sing, to shout, to beat-up somebody. He begins to laugh. He decides to have a girl.

144

'Hey! Boy!'

'Yessir.'

'Listen lad, where does a fellow have a bit of fun here?'

The man looked at him stupidly.

'I dunno, sir. Here I suppose?'

'Here! What do *you* call having a bit-of-fun, in God's name?'

'I dunno, sir. Good beer? Good wine? Eh?'

'You go to hell, you bastard! What do you do for women?'

'Oh? Women?'

'Yes! Women!'

The waiter leaned closer, and whispered. 'Is it . . . Are you asking . . . Do you mean the brothel?'

'What else? Yes.'

'Second on the left, first on the right, number fifteen.'

'That's more like it, laddie! For you.'

'Thank *you*, sir.'

He goes out, gets the wrong house, finds himself with three or four dressed-up women in a room, starts some horse-play, demands drink, sees his brother-in-law come in, cheers like a zany—So the old boy has some blood in him!—sees another old chap come in—It is M. the Minister!—cheers louder. General horror and confusion with the ladies in flight and the brother-in-law hammering him and screaming 'Canaille! Canaille! Canaille!'

Before considering what price has been paid for the effect obtained, consider the effect that has been obtained. One puts it down, not quite persuaded, yet quite amused. Afterwards it comes back to one more effectively, and it sticks in the memory like the taste of a sour sloe. It is raillery rather than humour. There is nothing objectionable about it. It is the fun of horse-play, of high spirits, and recalls those practical jokes that he loved to play on his friends. It is a caricature, a silhouette, a red-nosed mask. It has the merits of a caricature's spareness and speed—there is the laugh and you can laugh if you want-to. Above all it makes no pretensions—the premises were stated at the beginning, and we must have known that from those three simple or extrovert creatures no profound message would emerge.

None the less the reflective, the cultivated, and the sensitive reader will answer Maupassant's shrug with another shrug, meaning:

> I laugh, but so what? You have jeered away the life of a little town. After all, mon vieux, other writers have been amused at small-town life. Daudet; Mrs Gaskell; Mark Twain; Gogol; René Behaine; Chekov. They make us laugh without truculence, and even evoke an aftersigh of sympathy. Is there nothing at all to Madame Padoie and old Padoie but piety and stupidity and meanness? Have you not got your laugh a little too easily? Have you not, to use a vulgarism which is hardly likely to offend you, been more than a little bitchy?

What, again, could we fairly imagine Maupassant replying to that? He might easily be truculently contemptuous:

146

There are men like Varajou, brutes, bullies, call them extroverts if you want to be very refined, just as there are mean peasants and cowardly shopkeepers. You want me to keep a ledger of their bits and scraps of goodness, do you? You want me to say that they have their nice points, do you? Well, I suppose Varajou may have thrown a scrap to a dog, or given a whore an extra franc now and again. The hell with him and his craps and francs, and with British hypocrisy—always wanting to soften things down. 'We don't much care to discuss such people, Monsieur Maupassant.' I stand on the side of decency and straightforwardness. I like to see things as they generally are; you like to blink your eyes and be sentimental.

We may, for ourselves, make another observation, which applies to a great many of Maupassant's stories. It is that there are twenty ways of being realistic. When we say that he might have done this or that, are we saying what we would prefer or what would be better? Take 'Boule de Suif', that peak of Maupassant realism: the little whore who gave herself to the Prussian officer at the border in order to win his permission for the passage of the rest of her fellow-travellers. There is one element here which Maupassant has not mentioned, and which Mauriac, for example, would have had to mention. Mauriac would have remembered the rosary-beads and the pious pictures jumbled in prostitutes' purses with hard-earned fifty-franc notes and contraceptives. He would have felt compelled at least to mention the matter of mortal sin. But if he were to say that this element *ought* to be introduced his reasons would not be literary reasons, and many criticisms of Maupassant's work are, likewise, not so much literary criticisms as expressions of social or moral viewpoints, or, perhaps, of mere irrelevant personal taste.

If, then, I say that 'Une Soirée' is a thin story I must mean only that its effect is slight; or that the characters are thin, or that their affairs seem of little consequence to us, or that their misadventure is not very credible, though not impossible, or that it all adds up to a sufficiently amusing but trivial total. Chekov also wrote tales like this, 'funny stories', and they have been reprinted in his collected works. One would not say they were typical of his work.

Let us now take a middle-weight Maupassant story, that is to say one of his really good and more typical stories, though not of the first dozen: 'Le Diable'. This is a story of Norman peasant life. (And it is possibly true, as has often been said, that it is in his stories of Norman peasants that Maupassant did his most solid work.) An old peasant-woman is dying. Her son wants to sow the wheat and does not want to waste precious time watching by her death-bed. The doctor, furious at his avarice, forces him to go for the local corpse-washer and offer to pay her to watch by the dying woman. The son reluctantly goes to this woman, refuses to pay her by the day lest his mother should take too long about shutting her eyes, and demands, instead, a contract price. The sum agreed is six francs. The woman comes and the son goes to the fields. But, now, as the old mother lingers on and on the corpse-washer feels cheated, and the son seems to be smiling to himself. In despair the attendant begins to talk to the old woman about the Devil who, so she says, always visits the dying,

148

and having thus frightened her sufficiently she goes behind a curtain, dresses herself up fantastically, and making hideous noises, appears suddenly beside the bed, waving her arms and growling horribly. The old woman's heart leaps, she struggles to escape, and falls dead. All the last duties are thereupon performed carefully, methodically, and honourably, and everybody is content.

The force of this tale is inescapable. All Maupassant's disgust with life as he saw it among his Norman peasantry is packed into it. To the romantic—and romantics are never so romantic as when they are thinking about peasants—it is beastly, and they will refuse to admit that it is true.

Here we must at once stop ourselves from taking part in a foolish discussion. 'How true is it?' is not, and never can be, a fair question about any tale. Truth in literature is an aggregate, taken over the whole of a literature, and not even to be taken over the whole of any one writer's work—excepting always those three or four giants who, as I have insisted, must never be dragged into a discussion on the general run of literature. If we want to know the 'truth' about the French peasant we must read Maupassant, Bazin, Balzac, Bernanos, Mauriac, Beaumarchais, Mérimée, or such; just as, if we want to know the 'truth' about the English countryman, we must balance Hardy, George Eliot, Emily Brontë, Mark Rutherford, Mrs Gaskell, Fielding, Bates, Coppard and others. Which is why 'truth' in literature can only be protected, not by moralists, but by liberals who will allow it to flourish in variety rather than attempt to narrow it by compulsion.

What we may ask, in the presence of 'Le Diable', is not, 'How true is it?' but 'How persuasive is it?' The avarice of the Norman peasant seems to have hurt Maupassant deeply: he returns to it again and again. He sees this vice as riding their entire lives, a master theme that dominates everything, colours everything. We may grant it to him. We have to. As to persuasiveness, once again he has taken creatures of an uncomplex, elementary nature, from whom the most aboriginal sort of behaviour may be expected. That they had counter-balancing qualities we may suppose, and other stories of his give us reason to believe there were: such as 'Pierrot', to quote but one, which is about a dog that an old peasant woman was too mean to feed, and had enough heart not to want to kill. She dropped it down a hole into a cave where all the stray dogs of the region were thrown—until, horribly, in their hunger the stronger ultimately ate the weaker. Her natural decency led her, in her first revulsion of pity, to throw bits of food to Pierrot; still he howled; her avarice would not let her pay a man to go down and recover it; when she heard another bark, and knew that there were now two dogs in the cave, she abandoned Pierrot to his fate. There, at least, we have a struggle between avarice and decency. And, in 'Le Diable', the peasant did pay the corpse-washer to watch by his mother's bed; and before he went to sow his wheat he had asked his mother if he should not do so, and she, avaricious even when death is taking her hand, had feebly said that he must, of course, attend to the land. Are *these* nuances?

What one questions about Maupassant's stories is not what this or that one over-emphasizes or under-emphasizes: it is that the bulk of his work passes such an exclusively bitter and misanthropic judgment on life. He ignores all social and philosophic generalizations— those large conclusions and positions which assuage away the sharp detail of existence under benign or optimistic abstractions. Agreed that in doing so he is based on a position, himself; and that this position is almost piratical in its primitiveness; beyond and outside all those refinements, and elaborations, and disinfections of crude human nature that we call civilized life. For it is his satisfaction to peel off every shred of convention, in thought and action, and to reveal the elemental passions hidden but boiling beneath it. The elemental passions are his *métier*. Though there again is where we may wish to differ with him, since to him the elemental is almost always vulpine and it may be that a great many of his readers have found in elemental human nature the seeds of a nobler fire. However, Maupassant is not always on the side of the savage, and to prove this it is time I came to my third story, which I think one of his great tales, and which I have selected for this very reason that it shows him on his third plane of a realism that is still uncompromising but is not, at least as I read it, without sweetness and gentleness. It is 'Hautot Père et Fils'.

Hautot is a powerful, ruddy, bony old Norman, a man who could lift a whole cartload of apples on his back; half-peasant, half-gentleman, rich, respected, domineering, with a son, César, who is a quiet, gentle, obedient youth filled with respect for his father. With a couple of friends the father and son go out shooting one morning. The scene is brilliantly and swiftly painted, with three lines for the countryside and six for the sportsmen. At the end of the second page old

Hautot has met with the fatal accident; they find him holding his entrails into his belly. At the end of the third page he is in bed, alone with his sobbing son, confessing, through his racking death pains, that since his wife died some years ago he has had a mistress in Rouen:

'She's a fine girl. A grand girl. And if it wasn't for you, and thinking of your mother, and then this house— we've all lived here, the three of us—I'd have brought her here and married her. By God I would! Listen! Listen, boy! I could have made a will. But I didn't. A man mustn't write about things . . . I mean that sort of thing. . . . It's bad for the other children . . . it messes up everything . . . it's bad for everybody. All writs, legal papers, stamped papers. Bad! Never use 'em! If I'm rich it's because I never used 'em. Do you know what I'm talking about?'

'Yes, dad.'

'Listen. Carefully. What was it? I made no will. . . . I didn't want to. And I know you're a good lad. You're not tight, you're not mean. What? I said to myself, when I'm going, I'll tell him and ask him not to forget that poor little kid Caroline Donet. Rue de l'Eperlan. Eighteen. Third floor. The second door. Don't forget. Will you? And listen! When I'm gone, you go over to her, and fix it up so she won't have any grouse against me. You'll have all the cash now. You can do it. I'm leaving you enough. And listen! Go on a Thursday. That's the day she expects me. She works the rest of the week. Poor kid, she's going to have something to cry about. I'm telling all this to you because you're my son. A man doesn't tell this sort of yarn to a lawyer or

152

a priest. Nobody but the family in the secret. Family all one. Get me?'

'Yes, dad.'

'Promise?'

'Swear it?'

'Yes, dad.'

'Don't forget . . . I'm asking you. It's a favour. For God's sake. I'll hold you to it.'

'Yes, dad.'

'Go alone. You'll see . . . I can't tell you any more. On your oath?'

'Yes, dad . . .

He dies. Poor César weeps and weeps. And then, awkwardly, shyly, embarrassed, he goes to Rouen and seeks out the girl. When she opens the door she is astounded to see the son instead of the father, and when she hears the news she is overcome. In the flat there is also a little child who thinks this stranger is cruel to make its mamma weep so, and as César recounts every detail of his father's death the little boy kicks and kicks his shins. As he tells the whole story he looks around at his father's second home; the table ready; the wine warming; his chair; his picture; his little son. The three, full of sorrow, comfort one another. César fondles his little brother. He sees that Caroline is no hard-fisted strumpet: that she loved his father; that she cares little for his money. And since she *is* kind it is natural for her to force César to eat the meal simmering on the hob. When the time comes for them to part he finds that he has said nothing about money-matters. But he will come once again to fix all that up with her.

'If it's all the same to you, Monsieur César, can you come next Thursday? I don't lose any working-time that way. My Thursdays are always free.'

'All right. On Thursday.'

'Will you come in time for lunch?'

'Well, I don't know. I can't promise about that.'

'It's only that we can talk easier over the food. And it leaves us more time.'

'Very well then. At twelve.'

And off he goes, after kissing the little boy once more, and shaking hands with Mlle. Donet. He returns the next Thursday, and he has, indeed, in his misery and loneliness after his father's death, been rather looking forward to it. For she is evidently a very decent woman, and he cannot help thinking fondly of his little brother. He comes to her flat, kisses the child on both cheeks, shakes her hand, notices how pale and worn she is—the poor thing has been crying—and then over the meal he fixes everything just as his father has bade him to do, his heart full, a sense of his father about him, a sense of home. After coffee she begs him to smoke; he has forgotten his pipe; she hands him, from a cupboard, one of his father's pipes. As he smokes, and as she clears the table, he takes little Emile on his knee and plays horsey with him, listening to her in the kitchen tidying up the ware. At three he gets up to go, regretfully.

Here is how the story ends:

She stood before him, blushing, her heart moved, and as she looked at him she was thinking of the other man.

154

'Shan't we ever see one another, ever again?' she murmured. He replied, quite simply,

'Why, yes, if you like, mam'zelle.'

'Why, of course, I would like, Monsieur César. Say next Thursday, if that would suit you?'

'That suits me fine, Mam'zelle Donet.'

'And you *will* come to lunch?'

'But . . . Well, if you insist I won't say no.'

'That's agreed, then, Monsieur César. Next Thursday, at twelve, the same as today.'

'Thursday at twelve, Mam'zelle Donet.'

So the tale ends.

What is left out this time? Is there, indeed, anything? Or is it not a perfect story? Only one possible doubt may intrude: that Maupassant may not have written it quite as we may read it, or at any rate as I read it; he may not have intended the tenderness and softness, for example, which comes up to me from this tale like the warm breath of spring. He *may* have written it in the misanthropic mood in which he wrote so many of his earlier stories.

For here I must annotate this third choice and interpolate a few details of Maupassant's life-story. 'Hautot Père et Fils' comes from the volume called *La Main Gauche*, which is dated 1889. He was then thirty-nine. He died four years later. About this date a development of unexpected tenderness has been observed in his work. Perhaps even a little earlier, in his novel *Mont Oriol*, one might persuade oneself to see signs of a less brutal Maupassant, although I think one could only maintain the idea with some hardihood for 1889 and the arrival of the novel *Fort comme la Mort* and this volume of stories, *La Main Gauche*. Even then, tenderness may not be the word, or the note we observe. All I can say is that a new note has been observed widely, and mention that whereas Lemaître speaks of him as becoming 'plus fraternal, attentif, incliné' (more brotherly, considerate, well-disposed), Emile Faguet regards this new quality as 'une sorte de tristesse,' though still robust and masculine, and contrasts his earlier work and his later as that of a gay and a sombre pessimist. There was in his life at the time reason for both orientations: he was heartbroken when his brother Hervé, having gone slowly mad, died in an asylum, and he himself had cause to be uneasy as to his own fate. The same disease, which was to finish him too, was gaining control of his body; indeed when he was brought to Dr Blanche's private asylum at Passy, in a strait-jacket, in 1892, after trying to cut his throat at Cannes, one doctor there declared that he had been mad for two years, i.e. since 1890. The point (in literary criticism) is that, in 'Hautot Père et Fils', we are dealing with a story from a special period in its author's career. Whether more tender, or more *triste*, as one considers fit to call it, we have here Maupassant's realism softened by the addition of another note.

These, then, are three examples of Maupassant's realism, of its achievements and its limitations. We are now in a position to take one last story in order to balance both and so come to grips with our question as to how much he chose to pay for what he chose to win from life as literature. The question is a particularly interesting one for this reason, that although—as every reader of his stories knows—the marks of his realism are marks common to all realism, what he did was to

select the three main paths of the tradition, each naturally leading into the next one, and follow them farther
than anybody before or since. They are individualism,
scepticism and elementalism. He followed these three
roads or sections of the same road to the cliffs's edge,
there built his house, and faced the abyss.

<h1 style="text-align:center">4</h1>

Take them in order. The exit from classicism into
romanticism, like the exit from romanticism into realism, was the individualist assertion. It has been, indeed,
the beaten path of all modern thought from the French
Revolution to our own time. In prose fiction nobody
took this road as boldly and fearlessly as Maupassant.

What the individualist assertion has amounted to
in practice has been the alteration, almost the oblit-
eration, of the specific gravity of the mind, a lifting of
thought away from the hub or centre of established
order. This centripetal attraction of the centre is patent
in such a poet as Pope, or even a semi-romantic like
Chenier. (In England where the revolt came late the
centre functioned right up to our own day.) Writers in
this old tradition swing, however freely, or apparently
freely, about a fixed point. They present us always with
characters, ideas and emotions that gyrate about the
centre of gravity of a fixed morality. What the romantic
revolt did was to break this law of gravity so that thought
began to float away from the centre, and what one may
call generalized. Man began to fissurate into individual men. In another image, the atoms, once clustered
about a nucleus, fled apart, free, untrammelled, often

arrogantly self-assertive. Ever since, and in increasing discomfort and unease, we have become aware that although there is great joy and excitement and freedom in thus being free, disparate and mathematical, there are also great advantages and civilized rewards in unity of thought; indeed our greatest problem of today is how again to find cohesion plus variety, without falling into such extremes as Fascism or Communism or the traditionalism of a despotic church, the revolt from which foreshadowed the whole modern process four centuries ago.

Realism, as we know, was not at first, as Romanticism was not, a complete break. Balzac and Chekov, as we have seen, were intensely social men, and both were moralists. Not until the Naturalists took Realism a step further was the umbilical cord finally cut in literature, and many even of these naturalists or semi-naturalists (Daudet as a novelist, for example) still cherished the old traditional outlook. Flaubert's relentless *mépris du convenu* is the first clean cut, and Maupassant was his all-too-eager pupil. The preface to Maupassant's *Pierre et Jean* takes this individualism—and its accompanying scepticism—so far that in asserting his own individualistic 'realism' he denies all objective 'reality', quite without seeing the illogicality of his position and the subjective morass into which he has plunged:

> How childish moreover, [he says] to believe in 'reality' since we each carry our own reality in our thought and organs. Our eyes, our ears, our sense of smell, of taste, differing from one person to another, create as many truths as there are men on earth. And our minds, taking instruction from these organs, so

diversely impressed, understand, analyse and judge as if each of us belonged to a different race. Each one of us, therefore, forms for himself an illusion of the world which is poetic, sentimental, joyous, melancholy, unclean or dismal according to his nature. The writer has no other business than to reproduce faithfully this illusion with all the contrivances of art that he has learned or can command.

He then goes on to speak of these curious illusions of life:

The illusion of beauty, which is a human convention. The illusion of ugliness, which is a changing opinion. The illusion of truth, which is never immutable. The illusion of the ignoble, which attracts so many. The great artists are those who force humanity to accept their illusion. Let us not therefore get angry with any one theory since every theory is the generalized expression of a temperament asking itself questions.

Which is why he concludes that it is better that every man should paint what he sees and cut out all 'explanations', since in sum, no explanations are possible.

The distance which any fashion of thought can travel in twenty years is strikingly illustrated by this exaggeration of Flaubert's brand of Naturalism in the hands of Maupassant. Flaubert had been his teacher, his second father, welcoming him Sunday after Sunday for years to his home, reading his manuscripts, chiding him for their faults, encouraging him, making him come back again and again with new drafts. His influence was enormous and Maupassant acknowledged it fully and gratefully. In the main Flaubert's work was to disillusion him—if he needed disillusioning—about all conventional viewpoints; to open his eyes, *le deniaiser:* to impart to him his own relentless philosophy. But in that philosophy, even in Flaubert, even though it makes a chasm with traditional thought, there had still been a vestigial romantic streak, a lyric note that sweetens his realistic novels and floods out unrestrained in his romantic novels. This lyric note was rejected almost completely by the pupil. In those twenty years Naturalistic realism went to its limits, and beyond them. What died, in the meantime, as far as fiction was concerned, was free-will, the basis of the old psychology. The struggle between the will and the passions collapsed in favour of the passions. Love became desire. The most elementary forces now alone provided the tension, the drama and the pain. There occurred what Zola was to call the continuation in fiction of the physiology of science.

With this individualism and sceptism, sometimes hardening into determinism, went the lesser notes of naturalistic realism, such as the interest in the lives of common people, though as had been remarked, an interest little informed by that profound sympathy for the humble toiler which is the very soul of English realism, as, for example, in *Silas Marner, The Revolution in Tanner's Lane, David Copperfield, Jude the Obscure, Esther Waters,* or *The Old Wives' Tale.* The common people were not chosen out of affection but because in them the elemental was nearer the surface and because sophistication and convention did not have to be cut away, layer by layer, to get at it.

These are the most obvious marks of Maupassant's mind—individualism, scepticism, elementalism. To these, and to the general literary milieu, we can trace most of his individual technique, for, as cannot be said too often, literary technique does not exist in a vacuum, it is a man's device for projecting his own nature in his own time and place. Indeed, as Henry James shrewdly remarks, time and place affect even the technique of the reader as he reads, pointing out that not only does the impression of life that goes into a story vary according to the man and place that produces it, but the impression of life that comes out of a story will often vary 'according to the place that takes it, the particular structure and mixture of the recipient'.

To see, how, how Maupassant exhausts these three elements, let us turn to another of his stories and consider there just one of the characteristics of his method—his 'elementalist' refusal to indulge in elaborate psychology. Let us test this by one of his more feeling and more subtle tales, 'Miss Harriet'.

This is a sketch of an English woman of middle years, a tourist on holiday in a Norman seaside village. She is an evangelical Protestant; virginal; as we would say nowadays repressed; finding in her love of nature all the satisfaction that sex gives to others. She meets a painter, a gay young libertine, feels for him a painful emotion that throws her off her balance, is then so horrified and pained when she catches him locked in the arms of the servant-girl that she kills herself. It is a painful story and it must have given Maupassant a good deal of trouble to hold the reins, much more than it would have given to some writer who had not limited himself to such a severely laconic technique. For Henry James, or Turgenev, or Chekov would have expanded on the theme; they would have, so to speak, poetized it, sorrowed over it, been plangent over it, even allowed themselves at least a sub-audible comment, a suggestion of regret.

Maupassant handles his painful story with extreme cunning. To begin, he draws back a little from the scene; he sinks it into the personality of a narrator which is a useful, however risky, device whenever a theme is too crude or harsh for direct impact. Next he surrounds the theme with a more elaborate and lyrical atmosphere of natural beauty than is usual with him. We note, however, how spare and sharp his technique is in these natural descriptions. There is no description for description's sake; no luxuriating in irrelevant beauty.

> C'était l'automne. Des deux côtés du chemin les champs dénudés s'étendaient, jaunis par le pied court des avoines et des blés fauchés qui couvraient le sol comme une barbe mal rasée. La terre embrunée semblait fumer . . .

Turgenev could hardly have achieved in the same number of words this sensuous aspect of morning:

> Le soleil enfin se leva devant nous, tout rouge au bord de l'horizon: et, à mesure qu'il montait, plus clair de minute en minute, la campagne paraissait s'éveiller, sourire, se secouer, et ôter, comme une fille qui sort du lit, sa chemise de vapeurs blanches.

These notes occur in a brief preamble. Then the art-student tells his tale, in his own character. He appears as a *bon vivant*, yet not selfish, insensitive or

162

callous. The wandering student will, he says, pause where he feels attracted by a smell of clematis or by the naïve glance of a servant-girl in an inn.

But you must never make little of these tokens of country tenderness. These girls have a soul, they have their feelings, as well as firm cheeks and fresh lips. And their violent kisses are as sweet and as stinging as wild apples. Love is precious no matter where you find it. A heart that flutters when you appear, eyes that grow wet when you leave—these are too rare, too sweet, too dear to make little of them at any time.

This spontaneous note of natural affection is necessary to the tale. It is necessary for him to grow warm about lovemaking in a ditch, or a stable, or in hay still hot from the sun; to speak of coarse linen on soft skin; about the rough sincerity of country passions that can be more delicate than the subtle pleasures offered by charming and distinguished women of fashion. He must talk of the cold spring-water on moustache and nose-tip; of swimming naked in some icy pool; of the happy idle melancholy of the falling twilight. It helps to form a pagan contrast with the cold nature of Miss Harriet, his fellow-lodger in the little Breton inn.

She was thin, very tall, so tightly wrapped in a Scotch plaid shawl with red checks that you might think she had no arms at all if you did not see a long hand emerging at her side, holding a white tourist's sunshade. Her face was like a mummy's; it reminded me, I don't know why, of a red-herring wearing butterfly bows. She passed me swiftly, dropping her eyes, and retired into the chimney-corner.

Miss Harriet is one of those English travellers who leave in their wake a trail of educative or pious leaflets:

Who haunt the *tables d'hôtes* of Europe, spoil Italy, poison Switzerland . . . petrified virgins carrying with them the odours of their indescribable toilettes and a smell of rubber as if somebody slipped them at night into a sheath.

Whenever our student saw her he fled like a bird at the sight of a scarecrow.

But she had one frailty, if it can be called that. She was in love with nature.

Sometimes when I was painting among the rocks I would suddenly see her at the edge of a cliff as erect as a semaphore signal. She would be gazing, with passion, at the vast sea dusted with gold and at the sky purple with fire. Sometimes I would perceive her in a valley, walking fast, with her elastic English-woman's step; and I would come up with her, attracted by I don't know what, solely to see her visionary's face, her desiccated face, glowing with an interior and profound happiness.

Every reader and writer, will at once recognize here a wonderful subject for a short-story—a character, a situation and a promise, a Henry James situation. It develops as we expect. The painter paints 'her' cliff one day and in his enthusiasm for the picture shows it around. Miss Harriet looks at it in stupefaction, so moved that she speaks to him:

> 'Oh, monsieur, you understand nature in a most moving way.' I confess to you that I blushed, more affected by that compliment than if it had come from a queen. I was conquered, her victim, her slave. I could have kissed her.

At about this point the story of Miss Harriet begins to pass from the gentle hands of Henry James (or Turgenev) into the uncompromising hands of Maupassant. Never once does the young painter soften his coldly watchful eye. When she says, one gorgeous evening by the sea, that she wishes she were a little bird and could fly away into the firmament, the gushing remark is recorded coldly. He wishes only that he could have sketched her then and there for his album, a caricature of ecstasy. Pity is the only emotion permitted.

> Poor lonely creatures, poor wandering ghosts of the *table d'hôte*, poor, ridiculous, regrettable people, I love you because I once knew her.

She is by now evidently under his 'influence', using the word in its mesmeric sense. This gradual development is recorded with great intelligence and persuasive observation: the palpitations, the silences, the brusque speeches, the blushes, her furious pleasure when he gallantly and jocosely says, 'Why, you're as lovely as a star this evening, Miss Harriet'; her flights and returns; a crisis of nerves, a last revelation when he shows her

165

one of his best efforts and after looking at it for a long while she bursts into tears . . .

> I jumped up, stirred by the sight of this misery that I did not understand, and took her hands with a movement of sudden affection, the sort of thing a Frenchman will do quicker than he can think about it. For a few seconds she left her hands in mine and I felt them tremble as if all her nerves were being twisted. Then she pulled them from me, brusquely: rather she tore them away. I recognized that shivering. I'd felt it before. There is no mistaking that shiver of love in a woman, whether she is fifteen or fifty, whether she is poor or rich. It goes so straight for the heart that I always recognize it at once.

The direct physiological treatment has by now established the story as a Maupassant story. No other eye could compass this brusque and blunt observation of pitiable feminine weakness. The dénouement clinches the ownership of the tale like a label on a box. The young painter realizes that he must fly. He tells the aubergiste that evening he must leave. Miss Harriet does not flinch. But he catches the little maid, Celeste, looking at him. When he goes out after dinner, to smoke a pipe, he is stirred and troubled by the events of the day, the proposition of love directed at himself, passionately however grotesquely, bringing in train memories that charm and excite, and a certain gay humour roused in him by Celeste's quick glance. He is in a mood to do foolish things. All he does, in fact, is to seize Celeste in the dusk of the farmyard and shower her with kisses which she resists, laughingly, used to

166

these amorous assaults. It is all he does because Miss Harriet surprises them. She says nothing, flits away, and is not seen again. 'I went back into the house, much troubled, more embarrassed at having been surprised than if she had caught me in some criminal action.'

She has drowned herself. Nothing is spared in the description of the recovery of the poor, half-naked body and the preparation of this skinny corpse for the burial. ('My God, she *is* thin!') Pity is once more bestowed on her, the last kindness of wild flowers that the painter himself collects, and of his vigil through the night; and there is the bitter-sweet tribute of his thought that she will become part of the earth, of the God, whom she so loved:

She would decompose and become a part herself. She would bloom in the sun, be munched by the cattle, carried off by the birds as seed, and as the flesh of the beasts of the field would become human flesh again. But as for this thing they call the soul it was quenched in the depths of a dark pit. She would suffer no more. She had given her life to other lives who would be born of her.

Morning comes; the hours she adored:

I opened the window wide, drew the curtains so that the whole sky should see us, and leaning over the icy corpse I took her battered head in my palms and then, slowly, without fear, without any sense of disgust, I placed a kiss, a long kiss, on those lips that had never been kissed before.

167

There can scarcely be any need to underline the individualism, scepticism and elementalism of Maupassant's treatment of this unhappy theme; beyond, perhaps, the need to remark that it is unusually kind, for him, and that, before him, nobody except Flaubert would have dared either to select such a subject or to treat it with such cold unelaboration. I doubt if, even today, any writer would be either so cold in choice of subject or so laconic in treatment; certainly not the Americans, with all their supposed brutality, for when they deal with women they always reveal by sentimentality or savagery their emotional and sexual disturbance.

As to our specific point—Maupassant's refusal to indulge in elaborate psychology: somebody has called this picture of Miss Harriet 'a bizarre silhouette' and the adjective seems fair, but 'silhouette' is less just. The woman is persuasive; her emotions are sufficiently elaborate; her conflict sufficiently disturbing. What prompted the word was, probably, Maupassant's interest in elemental passion and his almost savage insistence on keeping to that plane. This is where he pursues his path to the cliff's edge, as he does consistently throughout his work. This is where he forces people to call him such names as *un Huron de génie*. This is where, at the end, we are in a position to appraise his power and measure his weakness—his price that he willingly pays, believing it to be not a weakness but a final and irrefragable strength.

The truth is that Maupassant saw life as a puritan moralist: he saw it, as he believed, without sentiment, and only with sensual eyes; he saw what a Christian would call the seven deadly sins, and he saw little else. He saw men and women ridden by pride, covetousness, lust, anger, gluttony, envy and sloth: Norman farmers, Parisian civil-servants, small-town bourgeoisie. What he denied was the slightest trace of soul in any one of them, the least speck of godliness, all hope of redemption here or hereafter. That was *his* reality, and it was in pursuit of it that he reduced human nature to its most elemental passions. Miss Harriet might be a Pantheist; she would die as a dog dies; the most that even an artist could strew on her grave was pity and flowers, and the thought that she would persist as a flower or as grass and as the flesh of an ox and the flesh of those after her who would eat her body and drink her blood. He reduced life to the senses and he revelled in them as a man and as a writer—not gaily, though he could be gay and did write gay, or at least gaily bitter, stories like 'Le Trou'. Before this philosophy of a Red Indian could ever weaken he would have had to suffer as terribly as a Red Indian under the torturer's knife and would he even then emit anything nearer to surrender than a groan? It is, therefore, more in anxious hope, I think, than in any real assurance that Lemaître wrote, though finely, that such realism as this has two great enemies, grief and death, and that in face of them it is futile to say that what is must be and that nothing needs to be explained:

> We suffer, and by that door of suffering there enters thought and wonder and disquiet and fear of the unknown and under one form or another reflection and dreams and the need to explain what the senses cannot compass.

169

Maupassant may have softened a little towards the end. The mass of his work is clean and classical in its raillery, its optimism, its stoical acceptance of a most ascetic and uncompromising view of life.

One's quarrel with such a writer, and one's admiration of him, will never be purely literary: they will be coloured by what, for short, one may call our philosophies, our own personal view of life, and we will approve or disapprove of Maupassant not as a writer but as a man with a similar, or with another (and unacceptable) view of life. It would not have troubled him, but the fact remains that he challenges such approvals and disapprovals more than any other writer of short stories. There is room in the house of Chekov, Stevenson or Henry James for men of many philosophies. Maupassant invites a select company or else a very tolerant one. That was his choice. He chose his way; he never diverged from it; he succeeded in it. He defined his own notion of reality early in his career—in 'Boule de Suif', his first published story; which is to say he defined his own temperament and its needs. When he had finished he looked into the abyss and it received him.

THE TECHNICAL STRUGGLE
SOLVITUR SCRIBENDO

5

ON CONVENTION

We forget when enjoying the pleasure of any art, of music, poetry, painting or the theatre, that a very great part of our pleasure has been dependent on convention. We are expected to forget it. In the theatre we have all tacitly agreed to see nothing odd about a room that, on the stage, lias only three sides; or, in painting, it does not seem odd to us that we see a view as if our heads were held in a vice whereas in life we let our eyes wander east and west, shift position a dozen times and see the landscape under fifty changing lights. The point is elementary; that is why it is so important; because it is so very obvious it is constantly forgotten, and this forgetting has, as I will show in this chapter, profound implications. I will here barely hint at one of them by recalling how a humorous philosopher once pointed to a cow in a field and said to me, 'What do you see there?' I obligingly said that I perceived a cow. 'But you do not,' he replied. 'You deduce a cow. All you see is the appearance of one-half of the outside of a cow. And when you look at a portrait of your aunt all you see is a picture of the outside of one-half of your aunt. You go through a series of lightning processes before accepting this superficies as a portrait of your aunt. It is, for instance, the whole case against Realism that it concentrates on giving us the outside of the one-half of everything.' In other words the convention of realism depends for its success on our forgetting that realism is a convention. So does every other convention.

The chief purpose of these conventions is, of course, the simple purpose of communication. Every art has its own hieroglyphics. These are its language, its technique, its conventions. In the short-story the speaker of this language is the writer; he has to learn its conventions, know what can be done with them, understand their limitations, adapt them to his own purpose, and often add to them. The listener to the language is the reader, and he, also, if he wants to get the most out of the art before him, has to familiarize himself with its conventions. The writer, however, must always presume that his reader is practised in these essential conventions, otherwise there can be no artistic communication at all. If therefore there is anything of a technical order which *can* be taught to would-be writers of the short-story it is in this field of accepted conventions. As in Bridge.

Let us take an example. One of these conventions concerns the beginnings of stories. A thousand years ago—or today in places like the Irish or Scottish highlands where the folk-mind is a thousand years old—a man could begin his story in this simple way, and nobody made the slightest demur:

Once upon a time, in a distant land, there lived a giant. This giant dwelt in a great castle on top of a mountain. He was the most powerful and dreaded giant in all that land. He had six arms and he had eyes at the back of his head as well as at the front, and when he roared the villagers a hundred miles away looked at the sky and said, 'The Thunder-Giant is angry today.'

Even that 'once-upon-a-time' was a convention, which meant that people agreed to believe the most fantastic impossibilities provided they occurred long ago and far away enough; and they did so for the sufficient reason that it amused them to do it. We still do this. Today, a story may begin like this, and, again, nobody will make the slightest demur. 'The underworld shivered. Word had gone out that Two-gun Hawkeye had escaped from Dartmoor and was on the loose again. For Hawk-eye was the man-eating spider at the centre of a vast network of criminal conspiracy that stretched from end to end of Europe. . . .' A business man who would refuse to pay fifteen shillings carriage on a gross of gentlemen's suspenders until he saw the invoice, will roll himself up like a dormouse in an armchair and swallow this whole, simply because it suits his pleasure.

As we become more sophisticated, however, we begin to nourish the tendency to disbelieve, so that the author has to make it all seem a little more plausible. We all know, for example, the story that begins with a preamble in which the writer tells us how he came into possession of the facts; for one of the natural concerns of every author is not merely to make fiction seem like authentic fact but to make us overlook his omniscience about it all, and omniscience reaching even to the secret thoughts and desires of complete strangers. He may begin, therefore, by telling us that he has found an old diary in an old chest in an attic, and that his story is based on that diary; or tell the whole story in the form of letters. Balzac's 'La Grande Bretèche' is pieced together from three conversations. Another device is to tell it all in the first person. One of the very loveliest short-stories ever written is 'Punin and Baburin' by Turgenev: it has the self-explanatory sub-title. 'Piotr Petrovich's Story', and not until Turgenev has written away two hundred and fifty precious words about his Piotr Petrovich do we come on the sentence, 'But I will begin my story consecutively and in proper order.' Inevitably that story runs to thirty-thousand words and is really not a short story at all.

Now one of the most successful inventions of the true modern short-story has been a convention which cuts out all that. Maupassant more than anybody else showed readers that if they were, as we say colloquially, 'quick on the uptake', they could dive into the narrative without any explanations, preambles, elaborate introductions, apologies, or other notations as to place, time or occasion. Thus 'La Parure' bluntly opens: 'She was one of those pretty and charming girls who . . .' We take this abrupt 'she' for granted nowadays. The convention has been established. Or take this opening to one of Thomas Hardy's short-stories—it is in *Life's Little Ironies*:—'To the eyes of a man viewing it from behind, the nut-brown hair was a wonder and a mystery . . .' In Defoe's time a reader would have said, 'What *is* he talking about?' Today we should have no difficulty in understanding a story that began at the end, e.g. 'The first thing Mullins knew after that was the nurse saying, "Feeling better now?" '

That is what I mean by the hieroglyphics of technique. It is shorthand, now an established device of convention, well-known to the merest amateur. Its main achievement is to shorten the preamble. 'Beginners,' says Chekov, 'have often to do this—fold in two and tear up the first half. Usually they try, as they saw, "to take you right into the story".' [Meaning the opposite.] 'So, the first half is superfluous. One must write so that the reader should understand, without the author's explanations . . . what it is all about.'

A further convention is inherent in this shorthand convention of abrupt openings, of which I have given examples: the technique of informing by means of suggestion or implication. Telling by means of suggestion or implication is one of the most important of all the modern short-story's shorthand conventions. It means that a short-story writer does not directly tell us things so much as let us guess or know them by implying them. The technical advantage is obvious. It takes a long time to tell anything directly and explicitly, it is a rather heavy-handed way of conveying information, and it does not arrest our imagination or hold our attention so firmly as when we get a subtle hint. Telling never dilates the mind with suggestion as implication does. Take the following example. It is the opening of Chekov's story 'The Lady with the Dog'. Here is the first sentence:—'It was reported that a new face had been seen on the quay; a lady with a little dog.'

The amount of information conveyed in that sentence is an interesting example of the shorthand of the modern short-story. What do we gather from it? 'It was reported that a new face had been seen on the quay; a lady with a little dog.' We gather, altogether by implication, that the scene is laid in a port. We gather that this port is a seaside resort, for ladies with little dogs do not perambulate on commercial docks. We gather that the season is fine weather—probably summer or autumn. We gather that this seaside resort is a sleepy, unfrequented little place: for one does not observe new faces at big, crowded places like Brighton or Deauville. Furthermore, the phrase 'it was reported' implies that gossip circulates in a friendly way at this sleepy resort. We gather still more. We gather that somebody has been bored and wakes up at this bit of gossip; and that we shall presently hear about him. I say 'him', because one again guesses, when it is a question of a lady, that the person most likely to be interested is a man. And sure enough the next sentence confirms all this. 'Dimitri Gomov who had been a fortnight at Yalta and got used to it . . .' And so on.

We may imagine how much time it would take, and how boring it would be to have all that told at length. This compression by suggestion and implication is one of the great charms of the modern short-story. And if the reader happens to be a person who wants to write short stories this is one of the first things to learn— that information must be conveyed in the most indirect manner possible. There is a famous example of this in one of Chekov's letters. He had been reading a story by a friend in which the moonlight was described at length in a highly poetic passage. 'No! No!' said the master. 'Not that way. If you want to describe the moon just mention that the old broken bottle on the side of the mill-dam was glinting in the moonlight.'

Some more examples. Consider Maupassant's 'La Parure'; about the poor civil-servant in the Department of Education, and his pretty wife who girds constantly at their poverty. Maupassant, to impress their poverty on us, mentions the food they eat, the simple and rarely- varied meals. When she brings in the inevitable *pot-au-feu,* or as we would say 'the Wednesday stew', the husband rubs his hands and says, 'Ah! The good old *pot-au-feu!*' Note that he does not say, 'What? Stew again!' He is quite pleased. We are to imagine by contrast with this easy-going satisfaction the greater exhaustion of his wife; his lack of spirit, of ambition, underlines her helplessness and hopelessness in being spanceled to such a long-suffering beast of burthen. If he had only said, 'God! I'm fed up with this blessed stew!' there might be some hope that out of that spark of rebellion something might happen. His dumb acquiescence emphasizes her despair. Of course a lazy reader will miss this implication: but, once more, every short-story writer must presume that his reader is not lazy but alert, or otherwise we could have no short-stories at all.

Take another sentence from the same story. 'She washed the dishes, using her rosy nails on the greasy pots and pans.' The word *rosy.* It is obvious how much pathetic misery the word conveys; but consider also how much else it implies. She will polish her pretty fingers in the evening; in the morning the dried grease on the pans will mock her efforts to keep the flag of her spirit flying. But she persists—she will polish them again and again. A story can be subtle in proportion as it manages to convey a greater and greater amount of information by means of these suggestions, and if a reader fails to catch the suggestions that is his loss.

Having made clear what is implied by the word convention I can now say that the short-story is itself one vast convention. There is in life no such thing as a short-story; all life's stories are long, long stories; or perhaps one may say that life is one long (or short) story; either way, to chop up life is to pretend that life is not continuous but spasmodic or intermittent. One may retort that life is episodical. The very word is a further convention, so long established that we do not realize it or have forgotten it. Is it an episode in our popular meaning of the word, i.e. something quite disjunct, when the cat dies or the cow calves or boy meets girl? It is the end of the cat's short-story, the beginning of the calf's, the middle of the cow's and the climax, or a climax, of the boy's and the girl's. If you retort that the death of your cat is an episode in your life I must be pedantic and insist that the episode, in its Greek meaning (which takes us back to the origin of the convention), is that which 'comes in besides'. Besides what? Aristotle's *Poetics* explains that episodes describe dramatically all that happens in between, or besides, the choric songs which give us the main continuity, and in whose continuity those episodes are a break or rift. In later drama the choruses dropped out (a prologue or epilogue their main vestiges) and the dramatic episodes remained, and either by their own poetry, or by inserted poetry, e.g. soliloquies, often felt as interruptions (thus reversing the process), sustained the continuity in another way.

All this has long been accepted, though often discussed, as for the novel. Nobody minds that a novel, instead of starting with, 'It was in the year 1900', should either begin in the middle of a man's life with, 'In the year 1920 a lone traveller might have been seen . . .' or, more abruptly, with ' "Yes, Mr Catchpole," said the tall man . . .' leaving us to decipher the characters and situation by degrees; and nobody minds either (much) if a novel 'ends' with, 'And Norma still sat singing on the balcony.' Perhaps this acceptance is easier because

180

there is a sort of notion that the novel is a long book like life—and an even more kindly notion that a very long novel is even more like life; and if a novel has a genealogical table and refers to several generations, still more so; while it may be felt that a series of novels, like Zola's Rougon-Macquart series, is almost as long as life itself. As for the ten thousand and one things that a man does and thinks during his day, not to mention during his life, which a novelist cannot be bothered with. . . . What the novel leaves out is then an old question and it is an old convention that all art leaves out something; such as the other half of my aunt and all her inside. Nor would it ever trouble anybody but an art critic that Italian painters before Caravaggio left out the sun, i.e. those dramatic Italian shadows that the sun slashed across everything they saw—but did not paint.

But if the novel, to keep to fiction, may omit so much, how much may the short-story omit—and pretend not to? For instance, the illusion of completeness and continuity can be easily created and sustained in a novel by reference to passing time, by movements from place to place, by incidental births and deaths, and so forth. With a short-story it is one of the anxieties of the writer that the episode shall *seem* more than an episode or disjunction. His devices to suggest this illusion are many.

I have spoken of the beginnings of stories; the ending of a short-story is one of the points where this problem of continuity will most acutely concern every writer. The one thing he must avoid is a sense of bump. We know, for example, the 'poetic' endings whose purpose is to float the narrative into the 'poetic' continuity of place whose image the reader will carry away in his thoughts, unaware of any sense of disjunction. Thus in Andreyev's story 'Silence' an unhappy girl commits suicide for no evident reason. Her harsh father is left in the torment of ignorance as to the reason. Andreyev feelingly describes the old man's efforts to make his wife speak, to make the girl's empty room speak, to make her grave speak. He is tortured by silence. The tale concludes, 'And silent was the dark, empty house.' Another Andreyev tale ends, 'A bluish light filtered through the curtained window and ushered in a new day.' A Gorki, story ends:

> Behind them rose the dark wood like a wall, murmuring softly to itself; the flames crackled merrily in the fire around which the silent shadows danced and an impenetrable darkness lay across the fields.

An Artsibashev tale ends, 'Over the broad fields the strong free wind blew evenly and sadly.' Daudet's lovely little story, 'The Pope Is Dead', ends:

> Thinking so, my eyes closed in spite of myself and I had visions of little boats painted in blue, stretches of the Saône made drowsy by the great heat, and the long legs of the water-spiders darting in every direction, marking the glassy surface of the river like diamonds.

These are slight tricks but they have a real use.

Then there are those endings which merge the episode into a general moral picture. Gauthier's 'The Pavilion on the Lake'. 'Did it make them happier? That we dare not affirm, for happiness is but a shadow in the

water.' De Musset's 'Camille'. ' "Now you see clearly,"
said Uncle Giraud, "that God pardons everything and
for ever." 'George Sand's 'The Marquise': ' "Well," she
said with a smile, "do you not believe now in the ideality
of the eighteenth century?" ' Victor Hugo's 'Claude
Gueux'. 'What Nature has begun in the individual
let society carry out. Look at Claude Gueuex. There
was a man . . . etc.' Balzac's 'The Christ in Flanders': '
"Belief," I said to myself, "is Life. I have just witnessed
the funeral of a monarchy, now we must defend the
Church." ' Balzac's 'A Passion in the Desert': 'In the
desert there is everything and there is nothing. . . . It
is God without man.'

Most writers of the short-story would probably
despise such easy and obvious devices to suggest continuity. There is a story by Chekov called 'Neighbours'
whose conclusion illustrates one of his favourite methods of evading the disjunctive bump. He, too, invokes
the 'poetic' mood of place and delicately he implies a
general idea or moral; he also suggests a favourite trick,
the present tense while using the past tense, and finally
he alludes to the prospect of the future.

From Koltovitch's copse and garden there came a
strong fragrant scent of lilies of the valley and hon-
ey-laden flowers. Pyotr Mihalitch rode along the
bank of the pond and looked mournfully into the
water. And thinking about his life he came to the
conclusion that he had never said or acted upon
what he really thought, and other people had repaid
him in the same way. And so the whole of life seemed
to him as dark as this water in which the night-sky

183

was reflected and water-weeds grew in a tangle. And it seemed to him that nothing could ever set it right.

This mood may be expressed as 'And so it goes on.' It is one of his favourite moods, and endings. So, 'Expensive Lessons':

She still comes to this day. Four books have already been translated but Vorotov knows no French but the word Mémoires, and when he is asked about his literary researches he waves his hand, and without answering turns the conversation to the weather.

This is the end of 'The Princess', where past tense merges at the end into a firm suggestion of present tense, and the typically Chekovian ironic comment is embedded in the last words:

The peasants she passed bowed to her, the carriage rustled softly, clouds of dust rose from under the wheels and floated over the golden rye, and it seemed to the princess that her body was swaying not on carriage cushions but on clouds, and that she herself was like a transparent little cloud . . . 'How happy I am,' she murmured shutting her eyes. 'How happy I am!'

Likewise 'The Chemist's Wife':

'Oh, how unhappy I am,' she repeated, suddenly melting into bitter tears. 'And nobody knows, nobody knows.'

'I forgot fourpence on the counter,' muttered the chemist, pulling the quilt over him. 'Put it away in the till, please.'

And at once he fell asleep again.

Present tense again in 'Ivan Matveyitch': 'He sits down and smiles broadly. Almost every evening he sits in this study and always feels . . . etc.' And in 'Zinotchka':

> . . . but still she did not treat me quite like a relation. And even now in spite of my good-humoured baldness, meek corpulence, and unassuming air, she still looks askance at me and . . . etc.

Let us not forget what all these illustrations illustrate. These are writers mesmerizing us into forgetfulness of the vastness of this convention which makes tiny bits of life speak for the whole of life.

As the form has become more and more known, of course, the convention needs less and less concealment; which brings us face to face with the *rationale* of all artistic conventions. It is dual. Firstly, if I leave out anything, even in a sentence, I am able to do so only on the presumption that my listener and I share a common mass of knowledge. If I say, 'Cat dead', I presume that he knows all that is necessary to know about cats and this cat. If I say at a pantomime, to calm a frightened child, 'Fake lion', I presume that he knows what a real lion is. This last example brings us to the second half of the matter; for we are, with this example, in the realm of fiction or pretence, and what I have said means that in fiction not merely do we share knowledge with the author but by tacit agreement we suppress it, or some of it. The child, that is, will enjoy the terror of watching the lion only when it knows that it is not a lion at all and tacitly agrees to suppress this knowledge. Our excitement at hearing a fatal shot on the stage is based on our suppressed knowledge that it is not a real shot, that the villain who falls dead is only an actor, and that he (unfortunately) is not dead. In simple words, we imagine, thanks to our knowledge of reality.

This is where the convention of Realism, so inadequately seen as a mere convention by most of those who practise it, asserts its complete artificiality. Chekov once offered a nice illustration of the purely conventional quality of Realism by pointing out that on the stage it is impossible to depict a death by poisoning as it would actually occur; but in order that it may nevertheless be done, he observes, in such a way that the onlookers will be satisfied that the dramatist knows what an actual death by poisoning does look like, there must be sufficient reference to scientific fact to set the onlooker at his ease. What does this mean? It means that in the old romantic convention a man on the stage died by poisoning without bothering about scientific fact. In *Hamlet* the queen drank the goblet, cried, 'O my dear Hamlet, I am poisoned', and flopped on the stage, stone-dead. The onlookers, that is to say, had accepted *that* convention. Today, our imaginations function less freely; we suspend our disbelief more grudgingly; but, in the end, we do suspend it; then in the same way as of old we use our imaginations and to just the same degree. The only difference lies in our *slowness* of imagination which must see a real gun before we will be pleased to forget that the shot it fires is all my eye and Betty Martin. Our

186

technical interest in this is that the important thing in Realism is not its supposed reality but something behind and beyond it. All those tricks for concluding stories are therefore merely ways of reminding us, at the end of a story, that there was more to it than met the eye.

Some of the best stories, however, blatantly chop up life, with 'bumps', and we agree not to mind, though it is probable that what we have actually agreed to accept is that all that was explicit in the older forms of the story is understood in the new: that 'so it goes on' (though there is now no need to say so); or that it is a moral tale, or a comment (though now there is no need to be explicit about it); or that it is 'typical', i.e. that it is a tale of, perhaps, Java or Italy but that it is a microcosm of everywhere.

From the point of view of these technical conventions there is one more thing to be said about the knowledge which writer shares with reader: some of it is suppressed, as I have shown, but some of it is very wideawake. When the poet wrote 'Hail to thee, blithe spirit, bird thou never wert', he presumed that we know what a skylark is, and that we know that he is not addressing an emanation but a normal man addressing a real bird, that we know that he knows that it is a bird although he says that it is not, that we understand that he knows quite well that the bird does not hear him, and that we nevertheless are likely to be pleased because our imagination is functioning thanks to its opposite, if knowledge of reality be the opposite of imagining an unreality. This is the suppressed knowledge basic to all convention. But the poet has ventured to presume much more. He must have presumed that he would be read by people who would at least not be completely at a loss before his fancy that Nature can sympathize with us and teach us: indeed he has used language which presumes an understanding of the most esoteric ideas, such as—'like an unbodied joy whose race is just begun'. He presumed that this overt understanding would function explicitly.

Every writer appeals therefore to a complex mass of emotions, of sensory experiences, of accepted, or acceptable ideas whose existence he presumes. If the reader cannot respond to this appeal out of his own experience he will not fully understand the writer. No boy, for instance, can fully understand the agony of the image of Joy putting its fingers to its lips and bidding adieu. Nobody who has not been bereaved can fully understand the anguish of the simple statement

> *But she is in her grave, and Oh,*
> *The difference to me.*

The writer, of short or long stories, making the brief part do for the whole, is thus referring in the shorthand of his art to a knowledge, sometimes suppressed, sometimes openly responding, which he both presumes to exist and hopes to enlarge. The more there is of the latter the more there is of the former. A freemasonry talks in passwords. And when readers reject a writer as false to life, as exaggerated, or even as unintelligible they may be right, but they may also simply be lacking in knowledge: they may be outsiders, like people who say golf is silly.

The supremely important technical point here is that while no writer can directly refer to more than is already half-perceived, he must, by every detail, *suggest* a whole 'idea' which may never be clearly perceived. Detail for its own sake is therefore pointless. Realism is only a veil and shadow of Reality.

Consider, now, in the light of all this the following two descriptions of women from two stories by Chekov. The first is, to me, quite meaningless. It appeals to nothing in me. It invokes no ulterior knowledge in me. It does not invite me to expand my knowledge. It does not invite me to imagine anything. It throws away the whole purpose of suggestion in a short-story because it does not suggest anything which it does not contain. It is the extract I have already given to show that Chekov has normally surpassed this level of Naturalism:

> On the top step of the old but lightly and softly carpeted staircase he was met by a maidservant with a haughty but not very youthful face . . . Exactly opposite the entrance he saw sitting in a big, low chair, such as old men use, a woman in an expensive Chinese dressing-gown, with her head wrapped up, leaning against a pillow. Nothing could be seen behind the woollen shawl in which she was muffled but a pale, long, pointed, somewhat aquiline nose, and one large dark eye. Her ample dressing-gown concealed her figure, but judging from her beautiful hand, from her voice, her nose and her eye, she might be twenty-six or twenty-eight.

Compare this with the description of 'The Lady with the Dog', noting how much fewer are the details and how suggestive they are:

She was a tall, erect woman with dark eyebrows, staid and dignified, and as she said of herself intellectual. She read a great deal, used phonetic spelling, called her husband not Dmitri but Dimitri, and he secretly considered her unintelligent, narrow, inelegant, and did not like to be at home.

I am invited to do a lot there: to see an original type, to plumb her character, to let my imagination expand her inward nature from a few outward signs. Or consider this description of the lady's husband, and not how Chekov again makes use of externals to suggest the inner nature of two men:

He bent his head at every step and seemed to be continually bowing. This was the husband whom, in a rush of bitter feeling, she once called a flunkey. And there really was in his long figure, his side-whiskers, and the small bald patch on his head, something of the flunkey's obsequiousness; his smile was sugary and in his buttonhole there was some badge of distinction like the number on a waiter.

I have said 'two men' for it is an interesting technical point that, in its place in the story, this outline has the double function of suggesting the nature of the man who is observed and of the man who, in watching this 'flunkey', is understood to have gathered the impression which I have just quoted. Generally, Chekov is, of all writers of short-stories, the most careful to use detail in this suggestive way, although, as I have said, he had a period when even he succumbed to the dull realism of the Zola school. The very word 'suggestive' comes into the few lines describing the impression which a young girl makes on one of his characters: 'Her expression was still childish and her figure was soft and slim: and her developed, girlish bosom, healthy and beautiful, was suggestive of Spring, real Spring.' What a charming use of realism that is.

Realistic detail, in short, is a bore if it merely gives us and idle verisimilitude: its function is to be part of this general revelation by suggestion. It is a fruitful realism when external reality releases the imagination: it is a barren realism when a reader says, 'I could almost see that tree; or smell that pond.' Why should anybody want *almost* to see a tree or smell a pond when he can go out in the fields and see a real tree and smell a real pond? Nowhere so much as in a short-story are such irrelevant descriptions out-of-place; there is no time for them: however striking they may be they are among the many things which have to be dropped in this general struggle to make a very tiny part do for the whole.

In the end that 'whole' is, of course, whatever a writer is 'getting at'. He has favourite themes, favourite subjects, favourite details to connote this, and when we come on them we subconsciously react to them, saying to ourselves, 'Ah! He's at it again.' What this 'it' is nobody can define; it is himself, his tang, his tingle, his personality, his *manière de voir*, and it may take him years and years to force that personal tingle on the public. The conventions by means of which he gets himself over to us are often invented by himself; they will be newer to us when we first meet his work, and they may be so simple or odd that we may not at first notice them, or quite understand them. Saroyan is one example. The first time I read a story by Saroyan he seemed to be merely wandering on and on. A great many of Henry James's first readers found it difficult to know what he was 'getting at'—and so do a great many of his later readers—but all now are prepared to slip softly into his sea and let his tingle wash over them. All this process of being 'washed over' comes from the same origin, that no artist nowadays will be objectively explicit in the manner of former artists. He is not interested in that sort of thing. All modern art has become more and more a sensation of communicated personality. Somebody like Mr Somerset Maugham would have sniffed furiously at this and said, 'I am content to entertain.' There is much to be said for this, especially since so many moderns (and ancients) have no personality worth communicating: but it has also to be said that there are many levels of 'entertainment', and that in fiction the more explicit one is the more one is likely to drop down and down to the level in painting of *A Hopeless Dawn, Derby Day,* or *Stag at Bay,* and in fiction to a realism as obvious and as pointless. You get a good yarn and that is all you get. I agree, however, that if a man has no special *manière de voir,* he had certainly better tell a yarn well than drool about his sensibilities. Far too many people with too much sensibility and no personality are playing at being writers (and painters) today.

I will give one more illustration of this convention of suggestion and be done. Characterization is something that can be no more than assumed in a short-story. If one looks for a detailed characterization one finds only puppets; one does not therefore look for it—another tacit agreement between author and reader. Instead we are given further hieroglyphics. We may, for example, be given situation, which always exposes some temperament or character; or conversation, which, if bright enough, reveals it; or gestures which express it, by which I do not mean that people make gestures—they are gestures, that and no more.

Turn to a story by a modern writer, Elizabeth Bowen. 'The Good Girl' is a characteristic story, among her best twelve. It is witty, malicious, intelligent, satirical, amusing. Uncle Porgie, who is not really an uncle, is Rolls-Royceing in Italy with his niece Monica, who is not his niece, and the lovely Dagmar who is not Monica's aunt though Captain Montparnesi is polite enough to pretend to think so. (We are left in no doubt as to Uncle Porgie's relations with Dagmar.) The Captain proposes to Monica who, rather helplessly, for she is a bit of a goose, permits an attachment, if not an engagement. One night she stays out late in his company—to the horror of Uncle Porgie, Dagmar and the proprietors of the hotel. Ladies and gentlemen do not do *this* sort of thing. Is not the hotel fully appointed? The gallant Captain disappears, having found that Monica is not an heiress. The 'good girl' is whirled off to Rome, very exhausted with Virtue, her own especially, and sadly sensible that it is her doom.

Now, the methods Miss Bowen employs to outline her characters—no short-story writer can do more—are of the swiftest. Monica has charm as well as virtue, we gather:

> Uncle Porgie, lifting his glass to twinkle in the pink lamplight, paid Monica tribute: 'She's a damn pretty girl and a good girl, too!' Yet, all the time under the table he had been pursuing Dagmar's foot.

It is almost a statement. She is a good girl whom one admires while playing footy with some other girl. That disposes of two characters. Captain Montparnesi is outlined brutally. He proposes, he kisses Monica's hands, she asks for time to think (she would), and when she has walked away: 'Captain Montparnesi brought his pocket-book from against his heart and made some calculations.' No more need be said.

The story can now proceed to display its wit and malice at its ease, and further minor elaborations of character may be picked up on the way, or not, according as the reader is alert or merely passing the time. Thus when Monica finishes reading a book on Leonardo da Vinci (poor child) she takes a walking stick and the hotel-dog (poor child) and walks down to the lake (poor child): if you do not bother to note the little stabs you will not murmur 'poor child.' At the end of her walk

she found mud-flats, washing, stark damp reeds, no one about. The lake was intended for distant scenery. She spoke Italian to a child who ran away, then she walked up again. On the terrace she had come upon Captain Montparnesi, engaged in sadness. He patted the dog. 'I love dogs,' he said: 'it is almost a passion with me.'

Naturally, he being a solitary man . . . and so on, with poor Monica gulping it all in. Or one may appreciate her natural resentment at Dagmar's smooth progress through the bewildering narrows of passion where she alone is lost; or Uncle Porgie's kindness in giving her a pair of coral ear-rings, since a good girl must have some compensations; or we may be amused by Captain Montparnesi's solemn family-council. But, whatever one does or does not find amusing and illuminating, one cannot fail to observe that this entire comedy creates its illusion with a minimum of characterization.

If anybody should imagine that this treatment of character is too, too simple, too, too puppet-like, he would do well to examine a story by even so masterly but leisurely a writer as Henry James. Take 'Owen Wingrave', the youth at the military crammers who suddenly rejects the army, for reasons of scruple, although descended from aeons of Wingraves who 'fell in battle'. (In no sense is it a short-story except that it ends abruptly; it unfolds itself rather than reveals itself.) We observe that the couple of pages of conversation which open the story reveal the temper of the youth and his crammer Mr Coyle. Then follows a page of leisurely Jamesian commentary on both. Notice with what an illusion of penetration these two puppets, these two 'gestures' are posed; with what elaboration they are pared to the skin:

> Mr Coyle was a professional coach: he prepared young men for the army, taking only three or four at a time, to whom he applied the irresistible stimulus of which the possession was both his secret and his fortune. He had not a great establishment; he would have said himself that it was not a wholesale business. Neither his system, his health nor his temper could have accommodated itself to numbers; so he weighed and measured his pupils and turned away more applicants than he passed. He was an artist in his line, caring only for picked subjects and capable

195

of sacrifices almost passionate for the individual. He liked ardent young men (there were kinds of capacity to which he was indifferent) and he had taken a particular fancy to Owen Wingrave . . .

I interrupt to insist that this is very finely said: but has very much really been said: We proceed:

. . . This young man's facility really fascinated him. His candidates usually did wonders and he might have sent up a multitude. He was a person of exactly the stature of Napoleon, with a certain flicker of genius in his light blue eyes; it had been said of him that he looked like a pianist. The tone of his favourite pupil now expressed, without intention indeed, a superior wisdom which irritated him. He had not especially suffered before from Wingrave's high opinion of himself, which had seemed justified by remarkable parts; but today it struck him as intolerable . . .

I cannot burthen the reader any further with this rather repetitious record. It is like a boxer who spars but won't fight. These are, evidently, fine spirits. They are presented to us with the true Jamesian delicacy. His grand manner is so impressive that, by reflection, these his children also impress us; we must feel that their feelings (such as they are) do them such great credit that it is almost bad manners on our part to observe that these characters are none the less just as flat and as puppet-like as any of Dickens's flattest characters. This is not, in the least, to find fault since they give us (unless we are as tiresomely critical as the present writer is doubtless being) a sufficient illusion of depth and roundness. Still, the only difference between them and any of Dickens's characters is that Dickens chose more vigorous and, perhaps, too explicit qualities and vices to emphasize—avarice, hypocrisy, optimism—whereas James generally chose more subtle and 'social' qualities which enlarged his characters by referring their elements to the sanctions of a select company.

I may suggest in passing that the reason why Dickens used flat characters or label-characters, is twofold; he had a great many characters to handle and had to stamp them clearly and simply; he also wrote serially, therefore episodically, and therefore became largely subject to the same limitations as the writers of short-stories who came after him. To one important point I will barely refer here. The instrument of characterization may be composed of no more than a couple of strings; it is the virtuosity of the writer to play subtle tunes upon this simple instrument. If the reader turns to the study of any dozen good examples he will see this for himself. We will, however, consider the point more fully in the chapters called 'On Subject' and 'On Construction'. For his own assurance he should study many examples of short-stories to test this matter of characterization: he will find that there is no time for explanation. The characterization of short-stories is always of the simplest. It is the cunning of the writer which conveys a contrary illusion, if he does.

The short-story, then, is an immense confidence-trick, an immense illusion, as immense a technical achievement as the performance of an adept magician. But there is no deception, or rather, the illusion here depends on our always knowing how it is done. The writer says, 'You observe, I have everything up my sleeve.' We wish, when we read for an epitome of Life we can have it only on certain, rather obvious, terms, and I have indicated a few of the terms. But there is one great difference between the two illusions. It is the height of the magician's art to make people appear to disappear; it is the height of this writer's art to make people appear to appear. The one does not really vanish and the other is also an illusion. It would be an embarrassment if the magician and his assistants pressed all the knobs and pulled the wires and arranged all the mirrors and if the lady in the cabinet still stood there as large as life. It is an even greater bore when short-story writers display an endless virtuosity and at the end of their performance the silk-hat is as empty as it was at the beginning

The purpose of all these tricks or conventions is to communicate personality while appearing only to 'tell a story'.

The most interesting thing to me about them is that they are so threadbare, few and obvious that I some-times doubt if there is any craft worth talking about in the short-story. For that matter, I believe that in all art about one-tenth is skill and the rest is personality. (Or call it genius. Or call it a mystery.) 'I have in me,' said Berlioz, 'a mysterious machine which I cannot control and which functions in a manner that I do not under-stand, and which I permit to function as it does only because I cannot prevent it from doing otherwise.'

6

ON SUBJECT

What subjects are suitable for short stories? To begin, I think if we examine some of the best stories of modern times in order to distinguish the essential and more valuable elements from the accidental and less valuable elements, we will find that the least essential element of all is the actual story or anecdote on which the tale hangs. For the moment, and for clear understanding, let us speak of this subject as the anecdote.

The anecdote is, in fact, the greatest tempter of the writer of stories. Take the example of that excellent anecdotal story of O. Henry's about the poor couple in New York. She had lovely golden hair: he had a golden watch. She was too poor to buy the rich Spanish comb she coveted; he was too poor to buy the watch-chain he desired. So, he and she, without telling one another, decided on a sacrifice. He sold his watch and bought her a lovely Spanish comb; meanwhile she went to the wig-maker, had her beautiful tresses cut, sold them to the wig-maker, and bought her beloved a watch-chain. Now one may well imagine how O. Henry rejoiced in that anecdote the first time he heard it or invented it. It is, deservedly, a famous story. It is nevertheless, by the highest tests, an inferior story—would that I had written it!—because the first time it is told it pleases you, the second time it is told you get less pleasure out of it (because there is nothing to it but the anecdote) and the third time it is told it bores you stiff. Whereas we can read a story by a master like Chekov or Henry James over and over again, where every turn is playing on the great instrument on which all stories worthy of the name, long or short, must play—the instrument of human nature—so various, so complex, so contradictory, so subtle, so amusing and so unexpected.

If one considers it, this is only natural. There is a primitive appeal in narrative, or anecdote. The earliest sagas contain little else; but as we develop we want to go a little deeper. A plain and simple record of incident, however heroic or amusing, could never satisfy the temper of our day. We have come to expect from the short-story much more than a series of incidents, however interesting they may be in themselves. Indeed this was probably always true among sophisticated readers. If, for example, we go back to the short stories of Boccaccio a great many of them may appear to consist wholly of an incident which is more or less—often less—surprising. But, if we weigh up Boccaccio we find that he did not win his reputation so easily: the lasting interest of Boccaccio is not the anecdote but the ironical comment of the whole collection of his *Decameron* on the foolish ways of human nature.

I think it is safe to say that unless a story makes this subtle comment on human nature, on the permanent relationships between people, their variety, their expectedness, and their unexpectedness, it is not a short-story in any modern sense. I can never be impressed by those people who tell us that the story of Jonah is a great short story, though, for its comment on human nature, I do believe that the story of Samson and Delilah is a great story. To put the matter quite simply, there is no reason on earth why any story should not contain an anecdote, and some of the greatest stories do, but an anecdote is not a story if that is all the story contains. In fact, it is an interesting matter to consider just how much anecdote even a good story can stand without appearing artificial.

Not until a writer has been a long time at his craft does he really harden his heart towards anecdotes. And I suspect that the reason why the practised writer avoids them is a wise reason: that the anecdote is a finished thing in itself, and that all that seems necessary is to get it down on paper at once. This in practice is what is wrong with it. A writer's mind is so much soil; an idea is the seed; the seed grows in his mind, swells and burgeons in his imagination; excites him as it stirs there, awakens other cells that stir and dance and form strange patterns and combinations, touch the cell of memory, the cells of desire, sets up in the uncharted geography of the brain a bubbling fermentation that finally overflows as the liquor of his art. It will have to be purified and matured and go through a whole lot of other painstaking processes after that—but there it is in its primal form. But the anecdote is already finished and complete! It is generally a husk, as far as its effects on the soil of the mind is concerned.

Over and over again one has this experience. Somebody comes to you bubbling with 'a good story'. At first one gets excited, and if the giver-of-gifts stopped there one might even still do something with the idea. But he goes on and on, developing, adding and completing, and the excitement evaporates slowly. What has happened is simply that he is not giving you an idea for a story at all. He has been giving you a finished thing, which, for months, he has been writing in speech; which may be why so often good talkers, good raconteurs rarely make good writers. Writing is done at the point of the pen, in private, a secret business—a private communion with one's own daemon. All writers, while they are writing, are cave-dwellers; witch-doctors; poteen-makers.

Let us turn for contrast with that anecdote of O. Henry's to the lovely story of Chekov's called 'Gooseberries'. Here, a civil servant dreams of the day when he will retire—as so many civil servants do. He will have a farm, a very little farm, just three or four acres, and a little cottage, and a gooseberry bush. The gooseberries become to him the symbol of the Simple Life. Time goes on, as time does, and he begins to amass rouble after rouble, as men do. But, then—and this is one of those unexpected touches with which human nature always surprises us—as the roubles accumulate the idealistic civil servant begins to get avaricious and ambitious. There is the first sly comment. Do not the dreams of youth always harden a little as we grow old? Lose their urgency, become in fact mere dreams—day dreams—deceiving us into constant procrastination? When we think of it do we not all know a dozen dreams of our own that we have silently discarded—so many little unrecorded defeats of the spirit?

So our civil servant gets older and older, and we find him marrying—not for love so much as for her money. And does this not suggest another comment on humanity—that it can fool itself into believing that the end justifies every means: so different from that noble ethic of the great Epicureans who held that the means justify the end? Presently the lady dies, and now the civil servant has a good deal of money, and at last he does retire, and he does buy a farm. But where has the Simple Life gone to? For it is an enormous farm; hundreds and hundreds of acres; and there is no gooseberry bush at all. (How the dream deceives us! Or rather how we deceive the dream!) However, he buys a score of gooseberry bushes and plants them, and one day his brother—who recounts the tale—comes to visit him, and finds him living in a very real sort of slatternly discomfort, the whole place shabby and untended—oh! very far from the simple dream in its pristine purity!—and they eat, and after the meal, in comes a plate of those symbolical gooseberries. They are the sourest, hardest, hairiest, toughest old gooseberries that Nature ever produced out of a cross between a rubber-tree and a cactus bush. But the face of the civil servant glows. He beams. He takes the sour fruit and as he savours it, it is plain that, at that moment, he is the happiest man on earth.

It is one of the loveliest of stories. So much irony; so much humour; so kind and understanding; and wrapped up in the most delicate poetic mood. It is probably one of the most perfect stories in the whole of the world's literature. At the end of it the brother moralizes—wondering how on earth people can so *deceive* themselves into being happy. Which gives the tale a double edge—for the brother is himself not happy; he has been cast into a most melancholy mood. By what? By the happiness of the man with the gooseberries. What is happipiness?—asks Chekov, with a kindly ironical smile on his face, inviting us to answer as we will but never to forget that human nature is like that, an instrument playing tricks on itself.

203

There, then, are two famous stories. One is anecdote worthy of the name. O. Henry has written a yarn—'a good one' as we say—perhaps a 'tall' story, perhaps in the after-dinner sense a good 'story', but not, in any reputable sense, what we mean by A Short Story. In practice, we have to come to make an easy distinction. We speak of stories like O. Henry's as commercial stories—and I think we all understand the significance of that definition. In a commercial story there is either no ultimate comment or it is as obvious as a kick from a mule.

It would, one must insist, however, be absurd to go too far here and say that there is no place in the short-story for anecdote; far from it. All one may insist on is that anecdote alone does not make a story, and that it has to be kept severely in its place. I do not even think that the short-story has come to absolute perfection in the hands of Chekov. I would not agree that what perfection he has achieved is the only kind of perfection; or deny that others have not written on other lines as finely as he did on this. His countryman, Gogol, for example; or Maupassant; or Robert Louis Stevenson. But I do believe that no writer of short-stories contradicts the fundamental principle about the very inferior importance of anecdote. To test this, let us take one of Maupassant's most famous tales which contains a well-turned anecdote: 'La Parure'.

Here we have another civil-servant, with a pretty little wife. They are poor, as, no doubt, civil servants occasionally are. And being pretty and young she wants to go to dances, and receptions, and mix with people from the Legations and so on, as even poor folk do. One day they get an invitation to an important function, a dance—and for the occasion she naturally wants to look her very best. She can make do with her best frock, but she has no jewels, and she fears that without them she will look just as poor as she is. So she borrows a diamond necklace from a rich school-friend, and delighted, off she goes to the dance and has a thoroughly happy time. When it is all over she has to wake up her husband—who has gone to sleep in an ante-room, as husbands will—they go out, get a cab, and off they go, back to their home.

But when she puts her hand to her throat to remove the necklace it is gone! She has lost those priceless diamonds. They go back; they search: they put advertisements in the paper. All in vain. She dare not face her rich friend without them, so what does she do? She goes to the best jeweller in the city and she buys, on the instalment system, an identical necklace. So, that one really happy night of her life becomes thereby the last happy night of her life; for now, their poverty is ten times worse than before: they are sunk under this load of debt; and for years and years the two poor creatures slave to pay for those diamonds. Her pretty looks go. Her hair dries up. The wrinkles come. And, then, after about ten years of this penury she meets her old school-friend once again and when her friend commiserates with her on her changed appearance, the once-pretty, still-plucky little woman says, proudly: 'It was all because of you.' And she recounts the sad tale. 'Oh, my dear child!' says her friend, in agony. 'But how unnecessary! Those diamonds were paste. I bought them for a few francs.'

Now, that is probably the most famous example in literature of what is known as the 'whip-crack ending'.

Those who like Chekov do not like it—it is so hard and so cruel. Personally, I do not particularly like it, but that, I realize, is a mere matter of taste and not of judgment. But the essential point is that this story would still be an excellent story, and some have even held that it would be a better story, if the thing stopped short with the slavery of the little wife and if there were no revelation about the diamonds being paste, no whip-crack ending at all. Those critics maintain that the whip-crack ending is too artificial, too unlikely, too ingenious. In any case, the real merits of the tale as read, do not lie in the cleverness of that ending. The tale has won its spurs long, long before we come to the ending. It has revealed a segment of society in which life is cruelly compressed and wounded. Those two people, man and wife, are real; their surroundings are real—real, perhaps, in a large typical way rather than in the individualized way which is Chekov's way. They evoke our pity. In short, the story makes its comment on human relationships; though in this case the relationship is social rather than personal. And as I said at the beginning, every story that is a story will, unconsciously, do that.[1]

The test is the old test. Can we re-read 'La Parure'? I think so; not as often perhaps, as we can re-read a story with greater shades and subtleties, but still as often as, in forgetting the anecdote, we wish to make acquaintance with that little pretty wife and her patient husband and wish to be reminded of all they stand for. But

[1]It is, of course, a very good point that *paste*-diamonds had made her happy. But I doubt if Maupassant meant this ironical comment on the nature of happiness.

we do not go back to it for the whip-crack ending, since the virtue of that ending ended when we first met it. We go back for the emotion which the seed of the idea created in Maupassant's mind long before the thought of the ending; and, in fact, it is pretty evident that the anecdote was a secondary thing to Maupassant's mind (if not an afterthought)—which apparently, is what the anecdotal part of every short-story has to be.

There is a simple way of demonstrating the inferior interest of the anecdote in any story. Restate it in a sentence and how banal it will appear. Thus Prosper Mérimée's 'Tamango' seems, in summary, merely to record how a shipload of slaves killed their masters and were, by hunger and disease, reduced to one, their black captor who had sold them in the first instance and then been shipped as a slave himself. Or suppose one were to say, 'I once read a story about a Frenchman lost in the desert who fell in love with a panther', would that suggest the mystery and force of Balzac's 'A Passion in the Desert'? Or could any summary even suggest (to one who had not read it) that Balzac's 'The Atheist's Mass' is one of his most impressive tales: as—'It is about an atheist who went to Mass four times a year for the repose of the soul of a poor man who had helped him in his youth.' Or:

> One day the monks in a monastery where a famous *liqueur* was distilled found that their father-distiller was drunk, and indeed, for their sakes, damning his soul in drink; however, they got over this by saying every night, on his behalf, the prayer of Saint Augustine to which is attached a plenary indulgence. (Daudet's 'The Elixir of Père Gaucher'.)

It is obvious that before any of these acorns can become trees two things must occur: the words will take flesh and the flesh will take after the father. In other words the created personalities will bring the fable alive and these personalities will seem projections of the creator's personality. The truth is that a writer imagines his subject into his own likeness. The subject of every story is therefore eternally virginal, eternally fructive. Nothing living has ever been written before. It is also true that every writer chooses (or imagines) like subjects all his life. Writers have a hundred wives and they are all after a pattern. It is not the subject that a man writes; it is himself. I cannot say it too often.

There is another test of the value of the ingenious anecdote. If we try to carry it forward a little beyond the point where the writer tends, so conveniently, to drop it we often find that its contrivance exposes itself. For example, the story of the little woman in 'La Parure' is not wholly tragic. Maupassant does not remind us that since she had given back a diamond necklace for a paste one she is now entitled to the diamonds, and is therefore, comparatively rich. It is, one may say, a small recompense; yet, the franc is such an important item in so many of Maupassant's other tales that one might well ask why he neglects it here. Likewise the O. Henry story which I have summarized need not have stopped where it did. Indeed it is, to a degree, a swindle. The girl's hair will grow again in a year and then she can wear the comb proudly and happily. Or she can return the comb, and he the watch-guard, and so buy back his watch and they will soon at least be where they were at the start of the tale. Realists are rarely as realist as they imagine.

All this leads us to observe, finally, that there are some fables which prove more solid than others as the basis of a story—fables that have none of the hollows that are always liable to occur wherever there is too much ingenuity. The strength of such simple subjects lies in the fact that the surprise they give us (usually a modest one) comes not from their complex contrivance but from the complex contrivance of human nature which they innocently reveal. To quote a modern example, I recall, with constant pleasure, a simple story by Ernst Ahlgren called 'Mother Malena's Hen'.

This tale concerned a hen which old Mother Malena kept in the poorhouse and which was a seed of continual dissension among the inmates. She has a rival, Pernilla, whose son, Nils, has a horrid and annoying way of mimicking and teasing the hen. (One must accept that this is all built up in an amusing and vivid way and that one really does feel, smell and see the poorhouse, with the two old women, the hen, the horrid boy, the little daily round, the comically vast dissensions arising from so small a cause.) One day Nils flings a stone at the hen, which flies to the woodpile and lies there to recover. The hen is thus 'lost'; not until it is lost do the poor old women realize that they had enjoyed bickering about the hen, and that Pernilla has been a cruel baiter of old Mother Malena, and that, in effect, they are bereaved and lonely without the hen. In a few days' time the hen staggers out of the woodpile; the joy of the old women is boundless; they have a feast to welcome the prodigal hen home, and all are reconciled.

The anecdote here is so innocent that when we apply our simple test of restating it in a sentence we find that it vanishes completely. Thus one might say:

'The old women in our poorhouse were always bickering about a hen belonging to one of them, until it was lost, and then they found that they had really enjoyed having it.' But, we observe, though the anecdote, such as it is, vanishes, the statement is not unmoving. Or if the reader finds it so I can only assure him that this is just the kind of sentence casually dropped in conversation, that sets the imagination of a story writer to work. He will see the women, begin to formulate the atmosphere, guess vaguely at the possible humour of the characterization, become eager to re-create the whole thing in his own terms. What will have interested him is not the incident—which had not been mentioned—but the play of personalities, and the accord between this human ballet and some music in his own head which is, so to speak, his theme-song. One can imagine him saying 'Yes, yes, this is the sort of thing *I* like.' In brief, he is choosing a subject (to quote Maupassant once again) 'in full concordance with all the tendencies of his thought'. Or, as I have said, he is writing himself.

The stories of Henry James are good possible illustrations of this. True, they are not, properly speaking, short-stories. It is true, also, that they are not light stories, by which I mean that the handling is somewhat ponderous—they give us the feeling that a very stately gentleman in a very ornate coat, gilded and tasselled and tailed, with fine calves of white silk, is approaching us with a cup of aromatic tea in elegant chinaware on a vast silver-salver. It is also true that there are few of his stories that a modern writer could not, to their advantage, reduce to at least half their length; mainly because he *tells* too much, i.e. has almost no power of

210

indirect suggestion.[1] But he does illustrate beautifully how much less important character is than incident; and he also makes for us the two distinctions which we have to make sooner or later, that situation is much more fructive than anecdote and that construction plus situation can supply all the plot we need.

Think of that amusing story 'The Real Thing'. Two elegant people, a man and wife, approach an artist explaining they wish to be painted. They are evidently of a type that James particularly likes, people with a splendid façade, of elegance and wordliness, which conceals poverty and vacuity; though they are nice people and we come to like their ingenuousness and simple decency. This pair wishes to be painted for money, as models. To cut this rather longish story short the painter (who potboils with illustrations for novels and magazines) finds that 'the real thing,' i.e. a real gentleman and a real lady, are too rigidly what they are to be good models for what they are. The perfect model for the gentlemanly type is an Italian ice-cream vendor, and for the lady a clever little Cockney slut, both of whom can suggest grace and elegance without freezing it into a convention. The point is subtle; its gradual elucidation keeps us in amused suspense; when Major Monarch and his wife are confronted with Miss Churm and Oronte the situation is ravishing. But, the concocter of stories will say—'What happens? Where's the plot?' There is none, in this sense. The story does contain, however, as readers of the story will vividly recall, all those elements which the word plot suggests, such as contrivance, situation,

[1] This will astound and infuriate his admirers. I, who am one myself, can only say, 'Go back to the short-stories and see.'

suspense, invention, action; or all except, perhaps (and this is the one thing editors and public most insist on), climax. Climax in, at any rate, the conventional sense has to be sacrificed to that deeper verisimilitude which is the conscience of the modern writer. In 'The Real Thing' what climax there is suffices; indeed it is searing to find Oronte and Miss Churm posing successfully as a gentleman and a lady while Major Monarch and his wife wash up the tea things.

It is, by contrast, almost painful when Henry James attempts, or is tempted by anecdote in the old sense; as in Taste'. There a dead parson's widow, once an actress, leaves behind her a quantity of stage-jewellery, which includes one valuable pearl necklace. Her step-son chooses, not unnaturally, to presume that, like the rest of the worthless stuff, the necklace is paste. The implications would otherwise be unpleasant. He hands over the entire heap of junk to his cousin. She discovers that the pearls are real and returns it to him, expecting him to persist, loyally, in denying that they are real. So he does. She next discovers that he has secretly sold them. One feels that the comment on the stepson's all-too-human nature is genuine, but that it has been at the price of an over-elaborate structure.

'The Pupil' is more pleasing, and more characteristic of Henry James's mind and technique. Here a tutor is employed by an apparently wealthy American family to coach their precocious but lovable child, Morgan. When the façade peels off gradually it appears that the tutor has fallen into the hands of a clutch of adventurers who rely on him to suffer penury and humiliation for the sake of his affectionate and sensitive pupil, who, it transpires, knows about his parents' shady technique of living, hates it and is ashamed of it. This is a wonderfully promising situation, though for a novel rather than a short-story. It ends with the final collapse of the rickety fortunes of the family and the death of the child: a climax, to be sure, but the climax of a novel rather than a short story. We can only be grateful that no effort has been made here to develop a plot: instead we move contentedly from one slight incident to another until it becomes evident that some catastrophe must bring down the house of cards, which is what so satisfactorily occurs.

The modern story-teller, then, has not dispensed with incident or anecdote or plot and all their concomitants, but he *has* changed their nature. There is still adventure; but it is now an adventure of the mind. There is suspense, but it is less a nervous suspense than an emotional or intellectual suspense. There is surprise, and plenty of it; but it is no longer the surprise of the man who opens a door and finds that a corpse falls out, but the surprise of a man who opens a cupboard and finds that a skeleton falls out. There is climax, but it is not the climax of the woman who discovers her lost jewels in the hatbox but the climax of the woman who discovers her lost happiness in a memory. There is contrivance, but it is not the contrivance of the gangster who deceives his enemy, but of the citizen who deceives his friend. A great stock-scene in the old-fashioned stories of adventure is when the hero unmasks the villain. It has become a stock-scene in the modern short-story when the author unmasks the hero; or it is one of the commonest themes of Chekov when the hero unmasks himself.

For all these things some incident is, of course, necessary: one of the best definitions ever given of the technique of fiction is that action reveals character, and that character demonstrates itself in action—and action is only another word for incident. But incident now is merely a trigger—a tiny piece of mechanism which explodes a projectile that smashes some façade, or explodes some concentration of laughter, fancy, tragedy, or delight. And while we enjoy the external pleasure of their vivid and rounded reality, yet it is surely not the mechanism we enjoy but the effect.

Let us take yet another example. There is a short story by Chekov called 'The Chorus Girl'. It has all the things that any story with an anecdote has; yet, in the old, accepted sense of the word, it cannot surely be said to have a plot and certainly not an anecdote.

In this tale we find Nikolay Kolpakov and his chorus-girl mistress, Pasha, suddenly startled by a knock on the door of her summer-bungalow where the two lovers are staying. He hides in the bedroom while Pasha opens the door. It is Kolpakov's wife come to inform Pasha that Kolpakov has embezzled nine hundred roubles and that the money must be replaced to avoid prosecution; Madame Kolpakov thereupon begs Pasha, emotionally and abusively, to give her the presents which her husband has presumably bought with the money so that she may replace it at once. Poor Pasha denies, truthfully, that she has ever received more than a few light baubles from the man, but she is harassed by the woman's tale and tears—Madame Kolpakov actually offers to go on her knees before the girl. Moved by the mother's picture of her children starving at home the chorus-girl finally and impulsively gives her every bit of jewellery she possesses. When Madame Kolpakov has gone away Kolpakov emerges, shaken and weeping at having seen his wife humiliate herself before his mistress.

> 'She! A Lady! So pure! So proud! Ready to go on her knees to a thing like you! And I brought her to this. I shall never forgive myself. Never! Go away, you slut! She'd have gone down on her two bended knees to *you*! O God forgive me!'

And contemptuously shoving Pasha aside he goes after his wife. Pasha already regrets her baubles, and flinging herself on the sofa begins to bawl. . . . So the story ends.

Can we say, by any stretch of the accepted meaning of the word, that this story is a plot-story? Yet, it has suspense, contrivance, climax, surprise, action, narrative. Let us, if necessary, call it a plot: but it is a plot in a quite new and purer meaning of the word. This refinement is one of the great achievements of the modern story.

'The Chorus Girl' is, incidentally, that typical Chekov theme—the unmasking theme. It is not an exposure of villainy. We are left wondering, rather, which character is at bottom the most decent: for all three of these unhappy people have revealed, in this trigger-incident of the husband's embezzlement, the admirable side of their natures—the loyalty of the wife, the impulsive generosity of the chorus-girl, even the husband's capacity for making some kind of honest admission of his own weakness; though he is, obviously, here merely a foil to the two women and is, indeed, a type commonly unmasked and mocked by Chekov.

The modern adventure, then, is an adventure through the jungle of human nature. Permanent relationships that human nature cannot deny, and cannot conceal, are found hidden away in the depths of the heart. Some incident like the final act of a play is taken by the author, and with it he fires his rocket into the air, and things otherwise hidden in the darkness are for a moment revealed in the sizzling light. If he is a pessimistic man with a sad view of human nature he will reveal the unpleasant things. It is necessary that we should remember them. If he is, like Chekov, a born optimist, his little starlight crackling overhead may show us the better side of humanity. It is necessary that we should never forget it. He makes no moral observation; he leaves that to us. If his incident had revealed none of these things he would have been like a child ringing the fire-alarm when there was no fire.

With these examples before us we may conveniently drop the word 'anecdote', replace it by the word 'incident', and apply to it an adjective that would have been meaningless earlier; we may speak of 'significant incident'—significant, that is, of some aspect of human relations or of the way personalities reveal comically or tragically some aspect of life which interests the writer. On such incidents the story-teller seizes joyfully. He has formed his image of life, desirable or undesirable; his notion of 'reality', pleasant or unpleasant, and in such incidents he finds corroboration for it. It may (we may now use our words a little less pedantically) be a very romantic sort of reality; his image of life may be high fantasy; he may love to see personalities, for instance, not so much reveal themselves in terms of psychology as transfigure themselves in terms of poetry; he may be a comic writer or a satirist and love to depict the bizarre side of human nature; or be a pure lyrist; even have less interest in individual personality than in personality generalized—I am thinking here of Ronald Firbank, and the reader will readily think of writers who illustrate the other types. In every case a chosen incident is significant to a writer for his notion of the way things are, as some wash of light on a landscape may make a moment and a place so significant to a painter that he will want to paint it at once, or as some quality in a woman may make her so desirable to one man that he must possess her, while leaving another man indifferent or even averse. And these writers will quarrel a little with each other, and may prefer, each one, his own notion of the way things are. But none will deny his friend's truth; he will merely assert the greater importance of his own—unless, like Maupassant, he is supremely arrogant, or, like Zola, a narrow doctrinaire.

The incident is, then, supremely important after all, though not to the story but to the story-teller. In theory any incident will do for the story; but only certain incidents will do for the writer. We can only hope to see why this is so when we read a short-story writer's work in bulk and begin to perceive that certain like incidents have appealed to him, at which point his literary personality may begin to emerge coherently in terms of his favourite situations or favourite types. We may see, too, that once the incident is embedded in the story its importance ceases, and that importance was and is purely subjective. Besides, in this the variety is endless and the nuances are not to be counted, and I have properly said only that we *may* observe a pattern, for it is a large hope and the writers themselves if asked why they chose certain incidents would be at a loss, being as a rule, and very naturally, unaware of their own prepossessions. Stevenson, for instance, had a very interesting prepossession. The Closed Door. Yet he does not mention it when speaking of the force of certain places and events. 'There is,' he says,

> a fitness in them; something we feel, should happen. We know what, yet we proceed in quest of it. Some places speak distinctly. Certain dank gardens cry out for a murder. Certain old houses demand to be haunted, and certain coasts are set apart for shipwreck.

We must add, on his behalf, that certain doors are fated to open on adventure; for he used this image, or symbol, or incident of The Closed Door with great effect more than once. He used it in that superb piece of outrageous romanticism, 'The Sire de Malétroit's Door', when a soldier fleeing from his pursuers presses back against a great oaken door in a dark alley and, on oiled hinges, it opens silently and closes automatically, holding the fugitive in an unknown darkness. He used The Closed Door in *Dr Jekyll and Mr Hyde*—that common door on the street, opening into Terror. It occurs in his story of François Villon, 'A Lodging for the Night'.

Chekov once picked up an ash-tray and said he could write a story about anything—even an ash-tray—but it is not true; and he never did write a story about an ashtray. He may have meant to convey something else; the cheerful advice which writers give to others is rarely intelligible, as when he also said, helpfully, 'One has simply to write about how Peter got married to Marie.' We do know what he is trying to say there: that we must choose simple subjects, and be unaffected about them;

one might as well tell a. young man in search of a wife to 'choose a simple girl and to be unaffected about her'. A fat lot of help that would be!

When I come to sum up what I have so far said about the subjects of short-stories, I find that I, too (in that, at least, like Chekov), have said little that is not of a very general nature; that any young writer will only waste his time and invite disappointments and court base temptation by poking about for ingenious situations, or composing clever plots, and then some day he will suddenly discover that in the innocence of his heart, which this kind of whoring after cleverness destroys, he has remembered something that moved him, written it down without affection, and found it good.

Is there no more particular and positive advice that one can give to a young writer on this matter of suitable Subject? Very little, and at any moment a practised writer is liable to disprove it. The stories of Henry James, for example, suggest one particular point very forcibly—that there are subjects which, of their nature, are unsuitable for short-stories. Since James, with constant arrogance, chose these subjects and used them successfully, all one can say is that these subjects are most suitable for writers of Henry James's calibre. None the less he also fails from time to time, and his successes are of varying merit. Consider two of his best tales—I have already mentioned them—'The Real Thing' and 'The Pupil'. The first is, in my opinion, both more successful and far more suited to short-story treatment because it lent itself to dramatic compression. This will become clearer when we are considering Construction; here it is enough to point to one element in the tale which automatically makes for dramatic compression—it is localized in one place, the artist's studio. For reasons that, I presume, are obvious this frame of place will always appeal to a writer of short-stories. The Pupil', on the contrary, is obliged to sprawl since the boy's family and the tutor must wander from capital to capital, and likewise it must sprawl in time. Evidently the sprawling theme is more suitable for a novel, though short-stories do, occasionally, take big leaps both in time and space. We are not surprised to find that inevitably 'The Pupil' took about twenty thousand words; 'The Real Thing' took about twelve thousand. A careful pruner could have reduced 'The Real Thing' to ten thousand without loss and without difficulty, and as I dare to try to show further on, it could have been cast in a form of about five thousand words.

The same is even more true of his delightful story 'Brooksmith'. Here there is only one character, the Admirable Crichton who had been unassumingly essential to the success of Oliver Offord's *salon*, but who had himself so enjoyed the company that, on Offord's death, he is unable to fit into any less distinguished home. There is, here too, as in 'The Real Thing', a natural frame of place, Offord's fireside. And had James been forced to write 'Brooksmith' for publication in a modern periodical I see no reason why he could not have discovered also a frame of time to keep the story within bounds. Both 'The Real Thing' and 'Brooksmith', that is to say, are natural short-story subjects; but 'Brooksmith' more so than 'The Real Thing', and either more so than 'The Pupil'. The result is that 'Brooksmith' fell into a mere eight thousand words or so, and a writer less given to indulging a constitutional, if not professorial loquacity could have written 'Brooksmith' in far less.

It is open to any devotee of Henry James to declare that he would not sacrifice one word of these delightful Jamesian amblings. Neither should I. But this has nothing to do with criticism. It is as when people declare that *The Shaving of Shagpat* is better than *The Egoist*, or that Peacock is the most pleasing novelist in English, or that Corvo is a better guide to Venice than Ruskin, or that San Stephano Rotondo is a more wonderful church than Saint Peter's—the sort of perverse affection that marks a weariness with all criticism, and the stage when one prefers personality to perfection. The fact remains that Henry James's short-stories are not short, and that some of them are so monstrously ill-constructed that if they were buildings they would have fallen down long ago, 'The Marriages', for example; and that what one often most enjoys about these discursive tales is their discursiveness, a quality hardly to be recommended in anybody else but, perhaps, Henry James, and certainly not to be commended generally in a book of criticism.

The outstanding weakness of Henry James's short-stories sums up a good deal of this chapter about Subject: he did not recognize enough that in short-story writing there can be no development of character. The most that can be done is to peel off an outer skin or mask, by means of an incident or two, in order to reveal that which is—as each writers sees this 'is'. The character will not change his spots; there is no time; if he seems likely to do so in the future the story can but glance at that future; if he seems likely to change at once, like Kolpakov in The Chorus Girl', we will have small reason to believe the change permanent. Naturally a writer will be attracted to subjects thus circumscribed and shirk subjects that require a series of incidents, or a prolonged

221

experience, as development of character always does. If he cannot avoid a subject which will involve the passage of time he will labour to enclose it in some other frame—place, for example. See one of James's best stories, 'A Man of Fifty', which is confined to Florence in order to compensate for the sprawl of time, and this time element is itself deceptively enclosed in the framework of a diary. Once development comes in, it increases a writer's task enormously and few can surmount the difficulties. That story of James is a magnificent exception.

We must be cautious, finally, when sitting at the feet of the great. There are charming tales that wander: Chekov's 'The Steppe'. A young writer might so fall in love with it as to find himself writing 'Steppes' for years. It is well to know that Chekov did not see 'The Steppe' as a short, or even a long, short-story, but as 'a series of tiny stories, set in one general frame'.[1] Nor would one take 'Gooseberries' as a model for a chapter of a novel because Chekov intended it to be that, any more than one would see as model short-stories those segments of novels which Henry James has presented to us under the guise of short-stories.

But it would appear that we are, imperceptibly, changing trains in our exploration of the short-story, and of Subject. We are, that is, beginning to think how subjects can be so handled as to make them 'suitable', and may as well admit the fact with a fresh chapter-heading.

---

[1] *Anton Chekov*. Trans. and edited by S. S. Koteliansky. Page 20. (Routledge, 1927)

7

ON CONSTRUCTION

Let us look over the shoulder of a writer of short-stories after he has chosen his subject; after he has started with his idea. The word 'idea' is not a good word but it will have to do. It may, as I have intimated, be a prepossession of some kind, some scene or character that excites him, something which, in a manner inexplicable to himself, has an almost symbolical significance in his mind. I have mentioned one of Stevenson's prepossessions, The Closed Door. Let us watch him at work on 'The Sire de Malétroit's Door'. He has got to the point where a soldier, fleeing from his pursuers, presses his back against a great oaken door and feels it, on oiled hinges, open silently and as silently close behind him, holding him imprisoned in an unknown darkness.

Let us watch Stevenson mould his principle about this image; by which I mean mould his idea of Life, as he himself had defined it, or made one of his characters in *The New Arabian Nights* define it: 'By Life I do not mean Thackeray's novels but the crimes and secret possibilities of our society and the principles of wise conduct among exceptional events.' It is the definition of a particular kind of romantic, or realist-romantic, but it is not very different to the ideas of other writers. It is mainly not a new idea but another literary vocabulary; for in 'exceptional events' we find 'incident' and in 'principles of wise conduct' we find that assertion of permanent 'human values', or that adumbration of a civilized idea of society to which Balzac or Chekov would have subscribed in other words but with like sense.

But, first, I must make one point quite clear. I have said 'mould his story . . .' I borrow that phrase from one of Stevenson's critics, Marcel Schwob. He said, 'As the smelter casts his bronze about the core of clay, Stevenson casts his story about the image he has called up.' This is an excellent phrase to describe the close construction of the short-story, because it means that the tale clings to the original idea. Clings! Let me seem to digress further, with a very simple example. The other day a young man sent me a story to read. An old man was dying, and as he approached, day after day, nearer to his end, he kept asking that his son should come to him. This son had been away from home, and, unknown to the old man, the boy had been killed. The wife persuaded a friend of the family, a young man of about the same build and colouring as her dead boy, to go upstairs and impersonate her son. The friend went upstairs, and the old man accepted him as his son. Now, so far, good. There is an idea and the story so far clings to it. But at the point the casting slowly broke. When he had gone down the old man told his wife that he had known in his heart all the time that his son was dead. At that completely disconnected anti-climax the story fell away from the idea and the whole casting was ruined.

A story follows step by step the main idea. In that story the story followed its idea up to the point where the old man accepted the impersonation. Everything had so far followed logically. It was conditioned by the first step. The wife, her dying man, her scheme, her plan, then . . . the stairs stop in mid-air, and by another stairs a hundred miles away, and entirely unconnected with the first stairs, we get quite a new idea, or angle, namely the second-sight of the old man. I felt at first that the trouble about that story was that the writer was uncertain as to his original image; so I asked him what he was driving at—what exactly it was that made him want to write it. Was it the old man, or his wife, or the impersonation, or what? To my surprise he said that what he was after was the contrast between the old man's vision of death and the quite human scheming of his wife—very much, for all its kind motivation, on the same plane as any wife's everyday scheming with any husband. This, I think, is a good poetic idea: this sudden sword of light thrust by Death down into the human, frail, workaday heart of petty life. It becomes apparent that, in that event, the weakness is that the bronze of the tale was cast about the wrong image. It was cast about the wife instead of about the husband. Naturally the tale does not 'cling'. A clever writer might, I agree, have inserted a contrapuntal technique between husband and wife. It would have given him a devil of a lot of trouble!

We may now come back to Stevenson's story 'The Sire de Malétroit's Door'. The young soldier has meanwhile been hesitating in the hallway behind the door. What next? Stevenson makes him explore the house, and in the first room that he enters he finds, to his amazement, an old man, who is the Sire de Malétroit, sitting waiting patiently for him. Now, this strikes us as both astonishing and absolutely right, because if the door was prepared it must have been prepared for some purpose, by somebody, and somebody astute and cunning enough to do it. True, the question uppermost in our minds is, 'How did the Sire de Malétroit know that, by chance, the young man would come at that very hour to that door of all doors in the town?' Therefore the tale must cling to this conundrum. The Sire de Malétrait, an unpleasantly leering old gentleman, tells the young man that *the* young lady is waiting for him, and presently she is introduced. The young man is further told that he must marry the lady before dawn—or die. The Sire de Malétroit retires and the young woman explains. She has been kept in that house as closely as if she were in a convent, but she has managed nevertheless to gain the attention and affection of a young officer in the town whom she had first seen at church. The unfortunate young hero of the story has been so unlucky as to come upon the door hitherto used nightly by this unknown lover. Her uncle has decided that she has disgraced him and that she shall marry her officer. A coincidence has been boldly foisted on us.

Stevenson has now got his characters into a first-class romantic situation. As we watch him proceed from this point we know that every step is crucial. One false note will wreck the story. But how is he to proceed? How is he to get his hero and this young woman out of the dilemma into which he has put them? First of all, the young soldier is the instrument. Secondly, the key-note is Romance. Thirdly, the atmosphere is Danger. The 'principle', by implication, is Honour and Happiness. For this story is a prologue-story, as I venture to call all romantic stories; as compared with the epilogue-story, which I apply as a convenient term to all tragic stories. This story does not end somebody's illusions. It begins them. We may, however, rely on Stevenson. He had, as somebody said, a great art of embroidery. His stories weave themselves into a tapestry of purple and scarlet and marigold. If it were only on style alone he is certain to carry it off.

But let us keep our eyes glued on the construction. The night passes. These two young people are alone. To save the lady's honour the young man has decided to refuse to marry her, which is highly romantic though rather inconvenient for everybody, not excluding Stevenson. Then, as both he and she look at the great cliff outside and think of the armed men waiting in the ante-rooms, their hearts are stirred towards one another, towards life, towards a great admiration on her part, and a great pity on his. There comes, just when it is emotionally due, the first touch of dawn—one of the most delicate descriptions of dawn in literature (and Stevenson was always excellent at natural description), and as it comes, the two young people are drawn irresistibly towards one another. By their love the problem is solved in honour and happiness.

There is no need to examine the tale more closely here, but it is well worth the reader's while to examine it at his leisure, and when he does re-read it he will see how closely the tale clings to the line of its original image. It moves from darkness to morning, from danger to salvation, from storm to calm, in tune throughout with its own impulse and the expectation that it arouses, as logical as a sonnet whose opening theme dictates its end, never divagating from its own character, and though it is not a closely compacted story—for that was not Stevenson's way—it is in every part wholly relevant to the original mood.

As to what final 'principles of wise conduct' emerge from this highly exceptional event I think it would be straining a point to extract them explicitly. What we get, rather, is a feeling of elevation such as we always get when we live vicariously through some gallant enterprise in which a man carries himself bravely. A fresh and happy light has been flung across the face of life. A bright wash of colour has been drawn over the landscape of experience. Human nature seems a little nobler. But we must not strain the point, and it is no more really than happens when we read any romantic tale, such as one of Scott's, or any story in which the sight of men acting and doing is always invigorating. The point is that there is some point, and that the story is built up, or constructed, to carry it like a pennant, and that without it 'The Sire de Malétroit's Door' would be merely a film-romance.

So much for the analysis, admittedly sketchy, of Stevenson's treatment of this subject. So analysed it looks straightforward and simple. 'Anybody could do it.' If he could think of it. But of what did Stevenson think? That we cannot know. What was the subject in the crudest alloy before Stevenson refined it to this perfection? That is the essential question about the construction of stories; not how a writer handles what one reads but what matter it was that he handled. What angle did the writer adopt to that matter? What line, what simplification, compression or distillation was it that made the subject fit into the mould of the short-story and so become a short-story? Perhaps the only answer is that given by Stevenson himself in *Memories and Portraits*, an answer which is sybilline but suggestive (I italicize the parts which seem to me the more suggestive):

> The threads of a story *come from time to time together and make a picture* in the web; the characters fall from time to time into *some attitude to each other or to nature*, which stamps the story home *like an illustration.* Crusoe recoiling from the footprint, Achilles shouting over against the Trojans, Ulysses bending the great bow, Christian running with his fingers in his ears—these are each *culminating moments in the legend* and each has been printed on the mind's eye for ever. . . . This, then, is the, plastic part of literature: *to embody character, thought or emotion in some act or attitude* that shall be remarkably striking to the mind's eye.

Sybilline, to us, because we would know what moment, which attitude, and which picture allured him in this tale, if, indeed, it 'came off' as he foresaw, and was not (as so often happens) replaced by some other arrangement which 'came together' or happily 'fell' into position, unplanned. At least, however, we see the dramatic approach, and the compactness that resulted, as distinct from the discursive way of, say, Henry James. It would seem, in fact, that because of this approach Stevenson might be considered a better writer of episodes than of novels, as James was certainly a better writer of novels than of episodes.

One element of Stevenson's story reminds us of what we saw in examining 'Owen Wingrave'. There is no real characterization. The two or three people here are noble, pathetic or wicked gestures rather than recognizable individuals. As we saw, Henry James and Elizabeth Bowen permit themselves some little outlines of character. That is the realist convention, just enough reality to assure us that Mr James and Miss Bowen are knowledgeable 'men of the world' and could expatiate further on character if they so wished. In this romantic convention situation does the work of characterization. It is always so in romance; there is rarely even an outline of character; for in romance, as Yeats said of tragic crises all character drops away and we are left with 'hard, gem-like flame'. True, realists as well as romantics exploit situation; but situation *alone* suffices for the romantic.

Balzac was almost a pure romantic when writing 'La Grande Bretèche' and he used therein nothing but situation to prise out his kernel. What his kernel is, who can say? As Sir Walter Raleigh put it, in writing about R.L.S., the kernel of a romantic story appeals 'to the blood . . . to the superstitions of the heart', never to the reason, and it is true that Balzac's story appeals to we know not what fears, hates, or 'anonymous desires and pleasures' (Stevenson's words). The Comte de Merret, the bald summary would run, discovers that his wife is unfaithful to him; taken one night by surprise her Spanish lover hides in a closet; the husband, having made the Countess swear that the closet is empty, bricks it up, and to all subsequent entreaties he replies coldly that she has sworn on the cross that the closet is empty. This is elemental drama; Elizabethan in its diabolism; or else it is a fairy-tale of Beauty and the Beast, or of an Ogre and a Damsel in Distress. Like much of Balzac the theme and the figures are more than life-size, more pathetic and more cruel than normal. (Which is typical of all romantics. 'Art,' says Thomas Hardy, 'is a disproportioning of realities.') A more natural woman, a more Flaubertian woman, might have fallen into the same situation as the Countess; but since no Flaubertian man would have handled it with the diabolism of the Comte de Merret, she would not have been so angelically helpless. Balzac presumably knew this as well as anybody else. He knew that he was handling something as primitive as a folk-tale. Here, certainly, all character falls away and passion burns blue, for there is no explaining emotions so primitive. Characterization is irrelevant here, even in the realist's outline. All one can do is re-create the mood, the atmosphere, affect the emotions and abandon rational persuasion.

It was this, I suggest, rather than the realist habit (though that, also was present) which made Balzac construct his tale in a manner that must, otherwise, be thought merely cumbersome. He first describes the abandoned château in all its mysterious gloom, isolation and decay; then the local lawyer who warns him to cease trespassing and reveals just a little of its strange story; then he describes how, in increasing curiosity, he tries to wheedle the whole tale from his landlady, and how she lifts another corner of the curtain, or, one is inclined to say, of the shroud. By this time we have heard of the death of the unhappy Comtesse de Merret, and of the unexplained disappearance of the Spanish refugee who had formerly stayed in this inn nearby. The narrator, having worked on our nerves and on our sympathy, finally prises from the maid Rosalie the secret of the Comte de Merret, and it is significant that Balzac does not recount this interview with the maid, as he has recounted his earlier interviews with the lawyer and the landlady, but, having created his atmosphere of awe, tells the story in straightforward narration. In all this from start to finish the only efforts to characterize the Comte and Comtesse are, for her, the bare adjectives 'kindhearted' and 'pleasant'; and for him, 'quicktempered', 'proud' and 'lively' and 'agreeable to women', adjectives so general that they might be applied to millions of men and women. All Balzac's labour has been concentrated elsewhere, on the creation of mood in preparation for the final situation.

One cannot say that the impressiveness of this tale lies wholly in this preliminary 'softening process', for the final tale is told with a very real dramatic power; but if we make the test of omitting all the preliminaries and going straight for the last four pages, beginning 'The room which Madame de Merret occupied at La Grande Bretèche was on the ground floor,' we will find that the effect is far less impressive. I do not say that this form of construction is neat, and I think that the realistic desire for external verisimilitude and plausibility has affected the construction, though it did not dictate it. Stevenson's story shows that it is by no means necessary to such stories. Other good examples of the method used in 'La Grande Bretèche' are Turgenev's 'Punin and Baburin'; the preamble to Chekov's 'Gooseberries' (which is linked with two other tales that should be read with it); Turgenev's 'The Brigadier'; or, to a lesser degree, Maupassant's 'Miss Harriet'.

Modern story-tellers have sought for greater compression than this. They aim to make situation and construction merge into a single movement and when they succeed they bring the short-story to its peak of technical achievement. Elizabeth Bowen's 'Her Table Spread' is a lovely example, in the romantic convention, of this merging. It compresses into the usual modern length of three thousand words material for which Turgenev would have needed twice or three times the space. The scene is Ireland, a castle on the coast, a rainy summer night, the candle-lit dinner table, a friendly party which includes the unromantic Mr Alban from London, whom the heiress Valeria Cuffe is vaguely expected to marry. In the bay there is a British destroyer whose ambience, all the more romantic by its nearness combined with its inaccessibility, emotionally disturbs them all. Valeria is especially affected. She is a very romantic young lady indeed who has, apparently, dreamed much of 'the Navy' and of marrying one Mr Garrett who had visited them the previous Easter, when another destroyer was anchored in the estuary. Mr Alban plays Mendelssohn, and then a Viennese waltz, while Valeria, now quite overbalanced, rushes out into the wet bushes to look at the misty portholes, and hug her dreams under the leaves in the moist night-air, and wave a mad lantern out to the rain-pocked sea. Her uncle and poor, abandoned, self-pitying, civilian Mr Alban go in agitation to the boat-house to search for her. There is a bottle of whisky in the boat and a bat in the rafters, and the uncle talks of marriage and the parlour-maid. The Irish are, it is evident to Mr Alban from London, just as dotty as people say. He flies from the bat and the bottle, and runs into Valeria, now beside herself, crying joyously that Mr Garret has landed; indeed Mr Alban *is* Mr Garrett. It becomes a moment when even Mr Alban is unmanned and manned, a fleeting mad moment of sheer abandonment to the excitement of the dark, wet summer's night, the creaking satin and the bare shoulders of the woman, a moment of rampant Celtic emotion. . . . The story concludes, or rather exhausts itself:

233

Perhaps it was best for them all that early, when next day first lightened the rain, the destroyer steamed out—below the extinguished Castle where Valeria lay with her arms wide, past the boat-house where Mr Rossiter lay insensible and the bat hung masked in its wings—down the estuary to the open sea.

The compression of this story is in such enormous degree due to the suggestive style (e.g. a word like 'extinguished' above, saves a whole phrase; or the word 'lightened', which gives a double sense of brightness and diminution) that we should keep this most difficult part of the analysis for our chapter 'On Language'. When we try to separate construction from situation the subtle management of the tale likewise resists dissection. I have long wondered whether the situation, the group, the place, or the atmosphere may have been felt first by the author; and whether Valeria came first, or Mr Alban, and felt that nobody would ever know, least of all the author; for the story has such thirst and urge that it looks as if it had sprung from Jove's forehead fully armed, complete when first conceived. When I asked Miss Bowen this question she said that she saw a castle like this and wanted at once to write 'something' about it; only a somewhat odd and rather dotty girl seemed to fit the mood of the place. The 'mood'? But whose mood? We are back at the indefinable; a writer's own personality seeing things in her own unique way.

One may appreciate the cohesion of 'Her Table Spread' by trying to imagine the story as Turgenev might have written it: the lonely girl (a), the remote place (b), the timid suitor (c), the anxious aunt (d), the Navy arriving (e)—step by step, leaf laid on delicate

234

leaf, lyric note on lyric note. Here all occurs together. The three unities of Place, Time and Character weld everything like a handgrip. For Place we keep to the castle dining-room, with a slight extension in lamplight to the garden (and for Mr Alban and Mr Rossiter a slightly wider but brief extension to the boat house), all but Mr Rossiter coming back to the dining-room for the climax. For Time, all occurs within about an hour, possibly two, except for the epilogue I have quoted, which passes to the following dawn. For character Alban is the focus. I cannot explain how much skill all this involves without a digression to what, for convenience, I call the technique of the camera-angle.

By camera-angle I mean the technique by which the writer of short-stories 'sights' his characters one by one without creating an uncomfortable feeling that we are wandering all over the cast; and without breaking the form of the story. As we read a short-story by Maupassant, or Chekov, or O. Henry, or Frank O'Connor, or Liam O'Flaherty, or A. E. Coppard—and as I mention the names a score or more of their stories pass quickly before me—we do not notice how the mental camera moves, withdraws to a distance to enclose a larger view, slips deftly from one character to another, while all the time holding one main direction of which these are only variations. This mobility as to the detail combined with the rigidity of the general direction is one of the great technical pleasures of the modern short-story.

One notes how, at the start, the writer decides on one character, or scene, for his general focus, e.g. in Stevenson's story the main character is the young man, Denis de Beaulieu. One may not note that while our attention is not deflected from him at any time in the course of the story several other characters join him from time to time unobtrusively; for it is only by a watchful re-reading of the story that one observes how gently these transitions are effected, and it is really only when one tries to write a short-story for oneself that one realizes how difficult it is not only to decide on the angle, but to make those variations on it.

Technically that story of Stevenson's is pretty elementary since nothing is easier than to make an entire story pass through the mind of one character, or to make one character the direct centre; which is how most stories are written. There are many interesting ways of doing it. I have underlined the fact that in the short-story suggestion is everything, and that direct telling is employed as little as possible. Likewise it becomes the highest craft in a tale if the angle is, to speak, concealed. Read for instance one of the finest of modern Irish short-stories, Frank O'Connor's 'In the Train'. This is a story about a woman who poisoned her husband. What is O'Connor's angle? He takes the story long after its obvious climax; he shows us the acquitted woman, the Guards, and the witnesses, all *coming back* in the train to their home. But within that general setting with what subtlety the camera slowly approaches, one might almost say coyly approaches, the central figure. We get glimpses of her through the minds of almost everybody else before at last the camera slews full face on to the woman the story is about. That is a beautiful piece of technique. Beside it, technically speaking, Stevenson's story is child's play. It is in such stories as 'In the Train' that the alertness of the reader, on which every short-story writer counts, is tested to the full, and I cannot say too often that the modern short-story is based on the most highly perfected technique in prose-fiction; and that we read short-stories not only for their matter or content but for the joy we get out of seeing a craftsman doing a delicate job of work. It would be the obvious thing, in O'Connor's story, to show us the woman actually in the thick of the crime. It would be less obvious to follow the crime through the course of the trial, and this device has frequently been employed. But what O'Connor was interested in was the kind of life the woman was going to lead in that little western village for the rest of her years. There, again, the obvious thing to do would be to depict her living that outcast life. Or it might be less so to show her as a very old woman, and to extract from her or from some friend in her old age, the story of her life. That device has also been employed. There are many ways in which the author might have fixed his camera. The time and position he chose, mid-way between the woman's past and future, in those few hours in the train joining her two lives, proposing her story as her friends and neighbours will see it, has the great merit of keeping a unity of time and place, a compact unity, while suggesting a large range of events and ideas.

This matter of the angle is paramount. It is a way of answering the question, 'What is the story about?' without being too obvious in the answer. So, I remember reading a story somewhere about a daughter which was really a story about the father, as did not appear until the last few lines. Or, in that story of Chekov's 'Gooseberries', the story was ostensibly about one man, and was so, but when we close the book we find that the narrator, the brother of the subject of the tale, has also unconsciously been revealing himself.

This kind of delayed action, this subtlety in the exposure, is not achieved easily, and no young writer of stories should attempt it at the start. He should be content if he succeeds in making his little human revelation in the simplest way, and as he becomes more sure of himself, and as his 'personality' becomes more complex the technique of construction will have to become subtle and complex also.

Having explained what I mean by camera-angle we can now come back to 'Her Table Spread', and observe how Elizabeth Bowen, while presenting a number of characters, has kept her Unity of Character. I have said that Alban is the focus. The story opens with him. 'Alban had few opinions on the subject of marriage . . .' When the other characters steal in to the story we may still feel that it is he who is observing them; some reaction from him is indicated in each paragraph to convey this impression of his pervasiveness. The fourth paragraph breaks into conversation, and the atmosphere of excitement is gradually released. Conversation is every writer's favourite way of escaping from his centre to his circumference. Everybody may share it. All overhear. The writer vanishes. And Mr Alban may see as well as hear. They have been speaking of the Navy's visit last Easter:

Will they remember? Valeria's bust was almost on the table. But with a rustle Mrs Treve pressed Valeria's toe. For the dining-room also looked out across the estuary, and the great girl had not once taken her eyes from the window. Perhaps it was unfortunate that Mr Alban should have coincided with the destroyer. Perhaps it was unfortunate for Mr Alban too. For he saw now he was less than half the feast . . .

That rustle of Mrs Treve's skirt is delicate. He could have heard that. One may presume that he looked up and saw Valeria staring out of the window. The next two sentences belong to anybody. Mrs Treve's thought? Guessed at by Mr Alban? They are interesting sentences, technically, because they illustrate how a writer may, having slipped his camera across a scene which includes the main character, quietly pick up other characters on the way. There is, as it were, an elastic bond of thought that ties up to the main character; we may stray from him quite a distance.

There is a nice example of this gentle truancy in the paragraph which follows; the reader will observe the sentence where we slip from Alban to their thoughts of him, and, later, where the writer slips in her own comment on him. (Valeria has meanwhile skipped out into the garden.)

In the drawing-room, empty of Valeria, the standard-lamps had been lit. Through their ballet-skirt shades, rose and lemon, they gave out a deep welcoming light. Alban, at the ladies' invitation, undraped the piano. He played, but they could see he was not pleased. It was obvious he had always been a civilian, and when he had taken his place on the piano-stool—which he twirled around three times rather fussily—his dinner-jacket wrinkled acoss his shoulders. It was sad they should feel indifferent, for he came from London. Mendelssohn was exasperating to them—they opened all four windows to let the music downhill. They preferred not to draw the curtains; the air, though damp, being pleasant tonight, they said.

To be sure, we do *not*, in reading for pleasure, observe anything very technical here. It would be obtrusive technique if we did. Indeed, it would not be technique at all since the function of technique is to create illusion, not to break illusion by poking its nose through it. There are hints and suggestions in that paragraph which we will quite unwittingly take; for example, they do not listen well—they get up in the middle of the music to open windows; they speak of the weather. There is more to it than that. They are troubled by Valeria's behaviour and seek to excuse it. 'The air is damp, but it's pleasant,' they said. It is natural for Valeria to have wished to stroll in it. This is true short-story writing; beautiful suggestibility all through.

The camera has stayed long enough away from Alban, so the next sentence returns full-face. 'The piano was damp but Alban played all his heart out . . .' etc. 'The piano was damp.' What compression of suggestion there! This is geniune poetic realism. Damp. The wet night. Neglect all round. The untended castle. And poor Alban playing his civilian heart out on the damp keys while they chatter. More general conversation allows the camera to wander again and this time the atmosphere becomes hysterical, and floating away on it, in the middle of a waltz played by Mr Alban (still, doubtless, brooding on himself, on her, on everything), Valeria is given the stage, racing past the window with her mad lantern. This is the most daring part of the story, and it comes off. She has robbed the stage from Alban and done it triumphantly. After two pages in which she and her crazy romantic dreams hold all our interest we return to Alban. He and the uncle go down to the boat-house in the rain after her and there is some secret drinking and maudlin chatter about marriage. When he flies from the boat-house he and she will rush into one another in the darkness, and she will take him into her dream and he will, in his woe and excitement, respond to her wild fancy and the climax will mount and topple. That moment is an emotional *tour de force*.

Not until we are thinking back on the story, perhaps days after, do we realize that it all began and ended with Mr Alban, and yet was called 'Her Table Spread'. It had been a story about a *girl's* romance all the time.

Naturally, Elizabeth Bowen was probably unaware of her own cleverness in all this; long practice, a gift of emotional combustibility, a great gift of words, an eye of a hawk, a special sympathy for the Valeria type—in one form or another Valeria turns up in all Miss Bowen's novels—combined to cast this perfectly fashioned story as freely and as unconsciously and as perfectly and as successfully as a fisherman casts his invisible line.

If one wishes for a criticism of comparison I suggest that one might read, after 'Her Table Spread', Henry James's 'The Beast in the Jungle'. If there ever was a waste of words here is utter squander. Everything is presented with an air of the greatest subtlety which, since the point is not subtle, can only make any normal reader resent the masculine self-importance of the presumption that we must approach the obvious on tiptoe. It is a tale about a gentleman who believes his solemn self to be fated for some appalling catastrophe. A kind woman agrees to watch beside him, through the years, for the coming of the Beast. She dies, telling him that the visitation has happened but that he will never know it. I really cannot say which must seem the more humorless, James in recounting (at great length), or I in repeating, that the Horror which this ass—the word is used early on with a brief flash of good-sense that lamentably disappears—has experienced in his failure to love the lady. He makes the momentous discovery in the last lines (about forty pages after the reader has presumed it), flinging himself with an appalling obviousness on his silly face across her tomb. Somebody like Oscar Wilde would have written the fable in a couple of thousand words, perhaps far less, and he would have done it simply by presuming that his readers had at least enough of his own mother-wit to be able to see a haystack without needing to be buried in it.

The stories of Henry James offer us many pleasures. One pleasure, to be expected of the short-story, which they do not offer is the eloquence of form. It is not merely that his stories are too discursive; in a sense they are not—in the sense that since he does not aim at form he may as well give us this other pleasure, and that no amount of pruning will therefore give us an alternative pleasure. Still, it would be possible to excise things that we might easily have presumed without being explicitly told them; such as passing personal comments irrelevant to the kernel of the tale, or illustrations, or elaborations which savour of self-indulgence, or even of sheer laziness. Thus, when he says that his two characters 'were visibly shy' we might be expected to gather this for ourselves; or when he says 'after all they were amateurs' this is something too obvious to need statement; and the largest pruning would remove a whole character and incident, the conversation with Hawley, a cumbersome piece of machinery which bursts apart the shape of the story, simply because James could not be bothered to convey the point which Hawley makes in a more subtle and economized way. Such pruning, which is quite different to the vulgarity of 'digesting', would come to a total of about six thousand words, and would reduce the story to about four thousand. But it does not give it literary form. Form is living and conceived, not subtracted or amputated.

'The Real Thing' might have been written in as many ways as there are writers to respond to the theme, but whoever should write it as a genuine short-story must see it in a framework of unity. James omitted only one thing. He placed it in the artist's studio from beginning to end, and saw it through the artist's eyes. This compactness pleases. He focused his camera clearly on Major and Mrs Monarch and this clarity is satisfying. The passage of time is not obtrusive though it is felt sufficiently to suggest a certain degree of sprawl. The reader will observe that there is virtually no characterization—Major and Mrs Monarch are little more than social types, nicely defined, though her kindness is evident, and in pruning one would be careful to leave in the incident of her rearrangement of the model's hair, since that is a nice and useful touch of character; and the loyal affection of husband and wife is also touching. This is quite enough characterization for the realist convention (a point I have fully dealt with in the chapter 'On Convention'). Situation is, as usual, necessary to fill in these light outlines, and the story is based on one of the happiest of situations. We have, therefore, almost everything requisite. All that is needed is that construction shall be added, or merged with, situation to give dramatic compression and eloquent form. This is the one thing missing. Henry James either would not or did not know how to construct his shorter tales into a satisfying form.

It must be said, however, that his stories have a special vertebrate quality of their own which, if not exactly form, is at any rate anatomy: he moulded the flesh about an *intellectual* idea. Perhaps he merely hung it on his idea? Here his idea is that 'the real thing', e.g. a real gentleman, may be such a conventional reality that it loses all the plastic quality of life. He may even be proposing that the lower orders, as represented by the Cockney and the Italian ice-cream vendor, have more plasticity because more reality? It will rest with each reader to measure the interest of this proposition which James chases hither and over like a retriever, though I am not sure that he does not also tend to chew the game. But though one may happen to have a strong personal liking for stories with an intelligent point to them the fact remains that point is not form. Henry James's stories dangle from his point like tapestry trailing from a hook.

Turgenev also liked to unfold his stories, but just when one begins to be a little oppressed by the long dangling scroll he will very quietly fold it up again. Think back on 'The Brigadier'. A narrator, an 'I', comes to fish and hunt in a remote country house; his host does not arrive for some days; in the interval he meets an old character, the Brigadier, whose story he unravels bit by bit—the story of a life well, or ill, lost for love. It is true that the narrative trails, but it does not trail more aimlessly than woodbine through the hedges, whereas the trailings of Henry James are old-man's-beard. Furthermore, the typical Turgenevian lyrical atmosphere hangs over it all, and at the end, when the friend arrives and an old key-letter from the Brigadier is produced it has the effect of a sad summary and recapitulation, a sort of fugal *da capo*. Finally there is a slight epilogue to murmur *Requiescat*. These are slight tricks, one may say. They are graceful. One appreciates their eloquence.

James, working in a somewhat similar leisurely way, does not make these efforts. Perhaps he prized his intellectualizations so much that they over-absorbed him? Recall the story once more. Major and Mrs Monarch come, ask for a sitting, are mistaken for patrons, prove to be models, and induce the artist to test them. The intellectual idea enters at once, with the 'real' model, Miss Churm. So does a new situation, or a restatement in even more intriguing terms of the old one, which has also the great merit of merging to two problems, the intellectual and the human. So far the movement of the story is perfect. All I would excise are some prolixities amounting to repetition; the 'cutting' process which any writer may legitimately do after his first draft. It is after this that the story begins to sprawl. There is too much by far about Miss Churm, and although the second, or Italian model is a defensible extra character on the grounds that he balances the Major as Miss Churm balances his wife, he is a mere repetition of the same idea. (He has great charm, and one would be sorry to lose him, but in short-stories one is always sorry to lose something or somebody.) But the Hawley intrusion is quite indefensible since it means that what should be integral to the situation is managed quite apart from it in a sort of choral interlude of some sixteen hundred words! It is also regrettable that we have to allow so much time to pass over our heads before we come to the point where it is realized that the 'real thing' is not so real after all. Unity of time and character have by this quite gone by the board and the sense of dramatic compression has evaporated under the benevolent sunning of the Jamesian style.

It can only be said that a more skilful, or a less indulgent writer would have laboured to compress the theme into, if it should be possible, a single occasion. For that Hawley must go, and either Miss Churm or Oronte should go, and the artist might come to his sad, and interesting, conclusion quickly. Some incident is demanded which will cap the situation so well arranged in the first two sections: or some further twist of character, such as (I throw out the suggestion more to illustrate what could be done than to suggest what might be done) a greater degree of perception in Mrs Monarch. It would help her to see, at once, face to face with the grace and suggestibility of Miss Churm that she and her husband would never do. It may be that it would have been wiser to focus the camera on her alone from the start. This is what I mean by saying that it is not a question of cutting to produce compression but of recasting the whole situation in terms of form; in short of tearing it all down and reconstructing it from the start. It would, of course, be stupid to have suggested this to Henry James. His temperament and talent were not of this order. Yet, it would not have been obtuse to point out to him that Turgenev, whom he so much admired, found ways of satisfying a temperament and exploiting a talent not inferior and not very different (the intellectual bent apart) to his own, while labouring equally on the shape as well as the content of his tales.

Before closing this chapter I must foresee one very natural criticism. Somebody may well say, 'What is all this elaborate nonsense about? Take any story by Hemingway and what part does all this wonderful technique play in it?' First of all, I confess that I have no great liking for the dissecting-room; though if there is no other way of demonstrating the skill and beauty of Nature's work it must be done. Secondly, not even a Hemingway can do without technique, though he may pare it to the bone. Read again that story of Hemingway's which is probably one of the best stories he ever wrote, 'The Light of the World'. It is the one about the three fat whores and the two peroxides in the station ticket-office, the homosexual cook who washed his hands in lemon juice, the three Indians, the Swedes and the hang-abouts who say nothing, and the two bums on whose behalf the story opens with the marvellous sentence: 'When he saw us come in the door the bartender looked up and then reached over and put the glass covers on the two free-lunch bowls.' While they all sit round, chaffing, somebody mentions one Steve Ketchel and one of the peroxides, hitherto silent, breaks into a histrionic thredody of praise and lamentation for the 'greatest, finest, whitest, most beautiful man that ever lived, Steve Ketchel, and his own father shot him down like a dog'. Whereat the fattest of all the whores, who had been shaking with laughter at everything up to this, begins to shake with tears, and a quarrel lights up between her and the peroxide, who, she says, is a dirty liar (as she obviously is) who never in her life layed Steve Ketchel. But Steve Ketchel, she sobs, did speak to me once. He said,

'You're a lovely piece, Alice.'

'He said it,' Alice said and smiled. 'And I remember when he said it, and I *was* lovely then exactly as he said, and right now I'm a better piece than you, you dried-up old hot-water bottle.'

'You can't insult me,' said Peroxide. 'You big mountain of pus. I have my memories. . . . Leave me with my memories, with my true, wonderful memories.'

So they quarrel over their past, miserably and unhappily, and everybody is moved and embarrassed. But Alice is smiling now, and the first bum sees that she is really pretty, and kind, and attractive and he believes in her. ('But my God she was big. She was as big as three women.') The second bum sees him looking at her and drags him away. That is all. A warm, human story, full of emotion.

Technique? Unity of place, a railway-station; of Time as long as it takes to tell; of Character, two bums. Characterization; nil. Poetry; full of it, unanalysable. Principle, idea, kernel, core, comment; it is in the title. Construction; two bums are thrown out of a bar and fall into a station, and fall out of it again, and pick up misery and pathos on the way. Form; in and out and in and out; as simple as could be. Suggestibility; nothing whatever is 'told', except for the first sentence, and that compresses two lives in two lines and three words. Subject; a whore's despairs? Nobody ever wrote a good story without as much technique as that.

But I am willing to agree that it is, perhaps, unnecessary to write a book to explain all this, and if some reader says that all one has to do in order to write short-stories is, apparently, to feel something desperately and to say it in the least possible number of words, I agree to that also.

I may have used too many words in saying so.

Two last elementary things are worth saying for the benefit of those younger readers and writers whom I have had much in mind when writing this book. The first is that I have found, in practice, that successful stories generally contain three elements or characters each of whose revolving light reveals the others. I say 'elements' because a memory might suffice, or a latent presence, even a symbolic object if it vibrates with enough force. It is also the function of one or other of the three to untie the situation. The second thing is, that I always like to feel that the author, when writing a story, is like the invisible, inobstrusive man in the projection box of a cinema, playing on a white screen where merging dots, lines, letters, words, images give the reader the illusion of watching, listening to, being with, finally of identifying himself with living people. If the author 'tells' instead of 'depicting', or if he 'explains' instead of mesmerically suggesting, he becomes like a fly passing across the beam of the projector in the cinema, magnified on the screen as an irritating intruder.

8

ON LANGUAGE

The short-story writer's problem of language is the
need for a speech which combines suggestion with
compression. One could underline the 'with', because
there is, of course, a great deal of suggestibility also
in the novel, but the effects aimed at are, as it were,
at artillery range. In the short tale it is hand-to-hand
fighting all the time: one may, to keep up the metaphor, win a height at the end of the struggle and see
a large perspective, but there can be little or no loose
movement up to that point. If I have to choose one
word to describe short-story language I would either
say that it is engrossed, or that it is alert.

At the very opening a writer, at any rate a modern
writer, must make an immediate and intimate contact
with his story. For this reason, I confess, I tend to judge
most of the stories I read by the opening sentences.
When I say this I am not thinking of beauty of phrase,
or the rhythm of the sentences, or anything of that sort.
I am thinking only of this one kind of effectiveness: do
we strike the key-note at once?

Hemingway's story which we have just looked at has
a perfect opening. Here is a caricature of the kind of
language which absolves one, immediately, from reading beyond the first two or three sentences. (Nor is it
very much of a caricature. These four sentences have

250

come from manuscripts sent to me by would-be writers of the short-story):

> The sun was tinged with gold. The perfume of the roses mingled with the warm heavy scent of evening. The last bird was warbling on a hawthorn. It was a breathtaking moment. . . .

Now, this is not merely atrocious English (we are not chiefly interested in that, for the moment), but it is also specifically quite unworkable as short-story English. In a novel it would still be atrocious, but it would not be unworkable, though admittedly on a low level. What is wrong with it is that it is not particular to any special occasion. It is not getting us anywhere. It is entirely general and vague; and a short-story is not a general or vague experience; it is isolated and special.

How could such language get anywhere! This warm, heavy scent of evening? What is this particular evening smell? Does one state some phenomenal incident in saying that the roses mingled their smell with this other smell, whatever it was? Are these rose-smells not already part of this general undefined smell? The writer is merely waving words vaguely around his head like a child with a veil at a suburban ballet-class. Can anyone *see* the sun 'tinged' with 'gold'? What dying gladiators of words! While as for 'warbling'! And 'breathtaking'! One can only advise such sinners to purchase Fowler's *Modern English Usage* and masticate such meaty bits as the articles on 'Novelese', 'Working and Stylish Words', 'Formal Words', 'Stock Pathos'—e.g. 'a lump in his throat'—and 'stricken', and so on. This general vagueness and fuzziness might—though not by any person

251

of discrimination—be tolerated in a novel where the mere interest of the anecdote induces one to read on for that entirely meretricious purpose of 'seeing what happened'; but a short-story has chosen to lift some particular and special experience out of the maze of life for *close* diagnosis, and no moment of life worth special experience could possibly be introduced by such sleepy slaves as those sentences.

There is something so unmistakably alert about the language of the short-story that we could not often, for instance, mistake the openings of short-stories (of even not-so-modern stories) for the openings of novels. Try it for yourself. Here are six openings; some of them are from short-stories, some from novels: and I may remark that it is quite difficult to give even tolerably fair examples, so obvious are the novelist's openings, such as: 'On the 15th of September 1840, about six o'clock in the morning, the *Ville-de-Montereau* was ready to sail from the Quai Saint-Bernard, and clouds of smoke were pouring from the funnel', which is the opening of Flaubert's *Sentimental Education*. Here are the six examples. As you read I invite you to say which opens a short-story and which a novel:

1. For several days on end remnants of the routed army had been passing through the town, mere crowds of disorderly fugitives that had once been soldiers.

2. The rambler who, for old association's sake, should trace the forsaken coach-road running almost in a meridional line from Bristol to the south shore of England, would find himself during the latter half

of his journey in the vicinity of some extensive woodlands, interspersed with apple-orchards.

3. Since the days of Adam there has been hardly a mischief done in this world but a woman has been at the bottom of it.

4. There they say, the three of them, Old Bertelsen and his two sons, Karl and Kristian, talking together in subdued voices.

5. The professor received a telegram from the Lyalikov's factory: he was asked to come as quickly as possible.

6. Take a smoky Western City. Call it Omaha or Kansas City or Denver, only let the Mississippi flow past it.

I am sure you will at least have picked out as novels, numbers two and six. You will be wrong, but not to be blamed for it. The second opening is from Hardy's *Woodlanders*; but the sixth is a short-story by a man not good at short-stories, and in essence a novelist, Theodore Dreiser, and his opening is a novelist's opening. Numbers one, four and five are characteristically nervous openings to short-stories. If you think the first not so nervous you might again feel justified, for it opens Maupassant's *long*-short-story 'Boule de Suif', and has just a shade of that story's leisureliness. There is one extract which is deceptive: the third, from *Barry Lyndon*. A short-story might well open that way, direct and to the point.

This eagerness to make immediate contact dictates something which may at first sight appear contradictory. It is that the style is retarded accordingly. The apparent contradiction will arise, if it does arise, from a confusion between alertness and speed. They are two different things. A man may be standing still and yet be alert. The immediate contact implies an intimate contact, and intimacy comes from alertness as to the value of detail and alertness as to the best way to exploit it. The inexperienced writer may think that in a short-story one must hurry since always at his back he hears Time's winged chariot; and there is so little Space. The contrary is true. The more space and time you have the faster you can go in fiction. The reason is simple: if you have much space, as in a novel, you will choose a large theme, probably have many characters, a complex design, and you have to get on with it. In a short-story one concentrates. Naturally the style is retarded. In a novel the effect is large and heavy and the mood establishes itself by an imperceptible mass-movement; all possible subtlety and delicacy notwithstanding. But although the whole mass moves as a mass, and so looks slow, it is really sweeping onward rapidly.

One may, it is true, build up a novel touch by touch; but the touches are farther apart since so much has to happen in between, and if one tries to put in too many the effect is breathless. One may want to wind oneself into every cranny, but these thrusts of event insistently block the crannies. We know the fate of novelists who deliberately hold up the event to describe minutely or to moralize: it is the Select Audience or else the Abridged Edition. One may wrap every chunk with sensibility and point it with the slyest intelligence;

it is the *chunk* that one so colours, not the detail inside the chunk. Let us see some examples.

Take this incident by Stephen Crane—the author of the famous 'The Open Boat' and 'The Red Badge of Courage'. It is from a story called 'The Monster', and describes how, during a fire, the acid on a laboratory bench topples over and drips on the face of an unconscious man lying on the floor. Note the slow style, as well as the accumulation of detail:

> There was a row of jars upon the top of this desk. For the most part they were silent amid this rioting, but there was one which seemed to hold a scintillant and rioting serpent.
>
> Suddenly the glass splintered, and a ruby-red snakelike thing poured its thick length out upon the top of the old desk. It coiled and hesitated, and then began to swim a languorous way down the mahogany slant. At the angle it waved its sizzling molten head to and fro over the closed eyes of the man beneath it. Then, in a moment, with a mystic impulse, it moved again, and the red snake flowed directly down into Johnson's upturned face.
>
> Afterwards the trail of this creature seemed to reek and amid flames and low explosions drops like red-hot jewels pattered softly down it at leisurely intervals.

A novelist employing so carefully incised an English as this would produce but few books; their movement would be of the slowest; and the effect would probably become intolerable after a time.

Compare this slow meticulous style with that of a novelist, even of a novelist who does load every rift with ore, who does caress her details, who makes every word work: the first page of Elizabeth Bowen's *The House in Paris*. Note that there is no lack of detail, but note, too, that, as I have said, the entire chunk is working towards the observation of the final sentence of the paragraph. For where the short-story writer seems to work with the sentence, and the word in it, the novelist works with the paragraph, or even with the chapter. Then note the unexpected thing, that the style in this unit is swifter than if there were less time and space:

There was just enough light to see. Henrietta, though dazed after her night journey, sat up straight in the taxi, looking out of the window. She had not left England before. She said to herself: This is Paris. The same streets, with implacably shut shops running into each other at odd angles, seemed to unreel past again and again. She thought she saw the same kiosks. Cafés were lit inside, chairs stacked on the tables: they were swabbing the floors. Men stood at a steamy counter drinking coffee. A woman came out with a tray of mimosa and the raw daylight fell on the yellow pollen: but for that there might have been no sky. These indifferent streets and early morning faces oppressed Henrietta, who was expecting to find Paris more gay and kind.

I have deliberately chosen a paragraph by one of the most subtle and sensitive modern prose-writers, whose novels are indeed, to be read almost with as much care as a short-story. Yet, even here, note the difference. Note the information conveyed—the sweep of the pure fact: that Henrietta has been travelling all night, is English, has not been in Paris before, and is touched by foreboding. Note, especially, that for the first two or three sentences that might be the opening of a short-story: but the paragraph moves quicker and quicker, and finally debouches, like an estuary, into the large expectation, or expansive delta of a novel. It is not that eel-trap on a weir with which a short-story closes in the attention to a fine point of some constricted, temporal and local preoccupation.

If we turn to almost any short-story by the same writer we note two things: the eel-trap or immediate convergence on the moment; and that the paragraph is not the unit here—the sentences are all of equal value. Take the opening paragraph of a story called 'The Little Girl's Room' in the volume *The Cat Jumps*. Word is laid on word, sentence on sentence; the writer is as completely engrossed as Stephen Crane was:

This is Geraldine's moment. At a nod from Mrs Letherton-Channing, carefully guarding the flame of her taper, she passed round the circle from cigarette to cigarette. The little girl's serious movements, the pretty shell of her hand, the soft braids of her hair as she stooped, swinging over her shoulders, the soft creak of her plaited sandals as she stepped, cast some kind of spell on the talk: silence followed her like a shadow.

At first Clara Ellis frowned: talk of a first-rate scandalous quality had been held up. But: 'Why,' she exclaimed, glancing at Geraldine's arm, 'you freckle just like a cowslip!'

'Do I?' blushed Geraldine . . .

By comparison with the novel, whose paragraph had so much completeness, we have got nowhere as to the action; yet, we are in the middle of the effect, to use Poe's word: though what that total effect will be we shall not know until the very end. The short-story is one elaborate self-contained chunk, and the language is engrossed to match.

How much engrossed? We hardly realize, today, so accustomed have we become to modern style, how far the process has gone.

Madame de Sévigné, we remember, said, 'Une feuille qui chante.' Not 'L'oiseau fait entendre sous le feuillage son chant joyeux.' The leaf sings. Language makes these leaps, of right, in poetry, by extension in prose; but only momentarily, under pressure of emotion. Normally, prose has, as I say, to get on with the job. Still, there are demands, even in prose, which evoke this dilation of language. When space presses, language speaks shorthand. The short-story makes this demand insistently, and readers, over the last fifty years, have come more and more insistently to demand it of writers. Readers are spry and knowing nowadays and do not like to be told things of which they can guess quite well, thank you. From this point of view of language Maupassant seems old-fashioned today. So does Chekov, if the English translations do justice to his Russian. It is a measure of the speed of this latter-day intensification of language that we can already read much of the earliest Joyce with a shock of surprise at the innocence of their style and the superficiality (in the literal sense of the surface-ness) of their English. He tells us things delicately but explicitly:

Night after night I had passed the house (it was vacation time) and studied the lighted square of window: and night after night I had found it lighted in the same way, faintly and evenly. If he was dead, I thought, I would see the reflection of candles on the darkened blind for I knew that two candles must be set at the head of a corpse . . .

When we read *Dubliners* long ago (first published in 1914) we had a different sensation. We admired the intensity, as we then thought, of the struggle to grapple with the shapes and faces of things, the vivid graphic quality of the descriptive detail. Today there is little of this kind of pleasure in his descriptions. They do not, we observe, grapple to compress, they peer and catalogue painstakingly, and the words are not always well-chosen:

> Ignatius Gallagher took off his hat and displayed a large closely-cropped head. His face was heavy, pale and clean-shaven. His eyes, which were of a bluish slate colour, relieved his unhealthy pallor and shone out plainly above the vivid orange tie he wore. Between these rival features the lips appeared very long and shapeless and colourless. He bent his head and felt with two sympathetic fingers the thin hair at the crown . . .

Is it true that Ignatius Gallagher 'displayed' his head? That word implies that he wished to show his baldness. 'His eyes . . . relieved his unhealthy pallor.' 'Rival features.' Is a tie a feature? The later Joyce must sometimes have smiled at this ingenuous English.

In the same volume we can find a comparison which shows both how language can be dilated or extended, and a foretaste of how Joyce would do it. Re-read the famous conclusion with an eye not on the meaning but on the choice of words which convey it:

> He watched sleepily the flakes, silver and dark, falling obliquely against the lamplight. The time had come for him to set out on his journey westward. Yes, the newspapers were right: snow was general all over Ireland. It was falling on every part of the dark central plain, on the treeless hills, falling softly upon the Bog of Allen and, farther westward, softly falling into the dark mutinous Shannon waves . . .

Knowing, now, Joyce's sensitiveness to the ultimate vibrations of words we might read too much subtlety into the passage; yet, even if we pretend to know nothing of the compression of the style of *Ulysses*, we may feel that the word 'obliquely' has a more than visual connotation, though the pictorial value of the oblique angle is, I agree, paramount and excellent.[1] We admire the risk successfully taken with the fine adjective 'mutinous waves'; for Joyce's danger, as this story alone would show, always was to be 'literary'. ('His soul had approached that region where dwell the vast hosts of the dead.' Soul . . . approached . . . region . . . where dwell . . . vast hosts. All bookish words; though breathed on.) We admire the lilt, another magnificently successful risk, which enlarges the value of the

[1] I mean that the word could suggest perversity and something of obliquity.

words. But one single word is most daring in the rest of this passage.

> It was falling, too, upon every part of the lonely churchyard on the hill where Michael Furey lay buried. It lay thickly drifted on the crooked crosses and head-stones, on the spears of the little gate, on the barren thorns. His soul swooned slowly as he heard the snow falling faintly through the universe and faintly falling, like the descent of their last end, upon all the living and the dead.

'Spears' is good, and 'swooned' has a charm, but the word on which I would pounce is 'descent', in 'the descent of their last end'. The word, which chimes with the image of descending snow, 'ascending to Heaven', 'the Lord will descend', etc. is taken out of its niche in the dictionary and given unique life.

One could find many other stray examples. In the dark streets 'a sound of low fugitive laughter made him tremble like a leaf'. 'She sat at the window watching the evening invade the avenue.' 'The high cold empty gloomy rooms liberated me.' 'A coachman shook music from the buckled harness.' Still, there were more similes than dilations, and most of what we had to admire was less a matter of language than of observation; not the force of 'he gnawed the rectitude of his life' but how 'the cabbage began to deposit a cold white grease on his plate' or 'the shapely cylinder' of a cigarette, or labourers in a pub 'dragging the sawdust over their spits with their heavy boots'—laborious words conveying what they contained and no more. In the later Joyce the interest shifts. Language is down beyond the Plimsoll line. He is less interested in direct picture-making. He deliberately sacrifices clarity to suggestibility.

In between *Dubliners* and *Finnegans Wake* English took on a more general liberty than we yet realize. One might expect this in romantic themes where the imagination itself is dilated. But even humorous writers may take these liberties. So, in V. S. Pritchett's 'The Chestnut Tree', a story which rivals the best scenes in Dickens, this is how we see the elder Miss Browne:

> Sometimes the elder Miss Browne sat beside Mr Drake, calling over the big ledgers. High on their stools these two looked like a King and a Queen. She had a romantic queenly air, sighed majestically or made little regal yawns behind her hands, sometimes stretching her arms to the back of her head and looking at us from a great, pale pillow of voluptuousness . . .

An impression of a picture, not a direct picture. He speaks of 'the white clouds smoking in the sky', or 'looking out into the leather darkness', 'the moon spinning on the tail of a dying wind'. Before the last war only somebody like Ronald Firbank would take these chances, and be called precious.

I do not suggest that short-story writers ought to use this sort of language—scores of excellent stories have been written in a more explicit language. But writers are now free to use it and to exploit it if they will, for readers will now co-operate with them if they ask for the extra attention needed; whereas Maupassant's readers, Chekov's, Ambrose Bierce's, Poe's would take such language in poetry only, or in a certain kind of privileged hierophantic prose. Poe's prose says everything; it proposes nothing other than the traditional meaning. And *how* traditional its metaphors and similes are! 'Death approaches and the shadow which fore-runs him has thrown a softening influence over my spirit.' 'In truth it was a dreamlike and soothing place, that venerable old town.' 'But the house!—how quaint an old building this was! (misprint: 'was this!')—to me how veritably a place of enchantment!' These sentences are from the opening pages and pages (and pages) of 'William Wilson'.

Here is the opening of Elizabeth Bowen's 'Her Table Spread', a story both humorous and romantic, its heroine unbalanced and its hero unmanned. What individual words in the opening passage strike us by their suggestiveness?

Alban had few opinions on the subject of marriage; his attitude to women was negative but in particular he was not attracted to Miss Cuffe. Coming down early for dinner, red satin dress cut low, she attacked the silence with loud laughter before he had spoken. He recollected having heard that she was abnormal—at twenty-five, of statuesque development, still detained in childhood . . .

For me the word 'red' seems deliberately chosen. It may, lightly, suggest Miss Cuffe's dramatic taste in dress. The word 'attacked' (the silence) suggests her strident personality; the word 'recollected' implies that Alban is disturbed, thinks back, perks up, is suddenly alert. The word 'detained' in childhood has ominous undertones as applied to this slightly batty lady. It suggests the doghouse.

This language of undertones is Miss Bowen's speciality. Thus, when Miss Cuffe becomes 'preoccupied' with attempts at gravity we may see her as looking even more vacant in her efforts to look less flighty. When Mr Alban begins to feel miserable by this 'indifferent shore' the adjective has a treble meaning—heedless, not so hopeless, quite hopeless. When Miss Cuffe proposes a row in the bay, rain or no rain, and the ladies 'produced indignation' we may feel that even these dotty Irish ladies are not wholly averse to the idea which they condemn; they have to force their indignation.

As the excitement mounts the language becomes more and more charged and less and less literal. Mr Alban's state of mind is proposed metaphorically.

Wandering among the apples and amphoras of an art school he had blundered into the life room; woman revolved gravely. 'Hell,' he said to the steps, mounting, his mind blank to the outcome.

Words now begin to extend freely, quite dilated.

Behind, through the windows, lamps spread great skirts of light, and Mars and Mercury, unable to contain themselves, stooped from their pedestals. . . . Close by Valeria's fingers creaked on her warm wet satin. She laughed like a princess, magnificently justified. Their unseen faces were all three lovely, and, in the silence after the laughter, such a strong tenderness reached him that, standing there in full manhood, he was for a moment not exiled. For the moment, without moving or speaking, he stood, in the dark, in a flame, as though all three said, 'My darling . . .'

Elsewhere in the story 'a smothered island' gives an immediate bosky effect without labouring for the picture. We see, or do not see, an 'extinguished Castle'. The striking image of 'The bat hung masked in its wings' is a sentence which gives the clue: this is the language of poetry magnificently taken over by prose. 'La poésie ne consiste pas,' says Saint Beuve, 'à tout dire mais à tout faire rêver.'

It is difficult to find a label for this modern use of English. Some of it is frankly neologistic. Some almost catachresis, or extravagant metaphor: cf. our now-common use of the word to 'jockey'; Miss Bowen's 'attacked' the silence. Most of it is what is technically known as radiation of meaning, which is not only legitimate but has always been the normal process of dilating language in poetry.

> By a succession of radiations the development of meaning may become almost infinitely complex. No dictionary can ever register a tithe of them, for, so long as language is alive, every speaker is constantly making new specialized amplifications of its words. . . . The limits of the definition must always be vague and even within these limits there is always scope for variety. If the speaker does not transgress these limits in a given instance we understand his meaning. . . . He has given us a conventional sign or symbol of his idea. Our interpretation of the sign will depend partly on the context, partly on what we know of the speaker, partly on the associations which we ourselves attach to the word . . .[1]

[1]Greenough and Kittredge, *Words and Their Ways in English Speech.* Chapter on 'Special Process'. (New York, 1926)

All these three elements are at work in the witty phrase 'detained in childhood', with its radiated meanings; that Miss Cuffe has got stuck (in the queue) is engaged (in the nursery), has not been allowed to proceed (by Nursery), or is already in the Big house.

It may be said that such use of language does not make for clarity; it does not. Neither does it make pictures; it is impressionistic, in letters a special feminine strength or weakness. It makes stringent demands on the wit and the intelligence lest it became just too, too clever or an end in itself, or 'trangress the limits'. Yet in this language some of the wittiest things in English have been written and without it we should not have had the romantic music of such as Carlyle or Browne. Its value for the writer of short-stories is at least indisputable in one respect: so alert a language helps to make short-stories shorter.

The opposite kind of language whose words are more precise, literal and factual is generally, at least hitherto, found in realistic fiction. It is a more ponderous English, and naturally so since every word conveys but one sense, as opposed to the variety of senses suggested by 'radiated' English, and these conscientious words sway in long strides from tip to tail of a sentence like the camels of a caravan, very much, indeed, after the manner of this sentence I am now writing. Not to suggest that the one language is 'better' or 'less interesting' than the other, but to make clear that the two styles are quite different. I will end by quoting a few sentences from a good modern writer of realism, Mr William Sansom. The sentences are taken from his story 'The Boiler Room', and I think they well illustrate how this style of realistic subject and treatment almost inevitably invites a correspondingly factual and unsuggestive English:

> The two big boilers stood side by side, separated by a few feet and a protective railing. Their massive round iron sides were rusted brown and then greyed over with dust, but the railings encircling them had been painted bright green, so that in their rough-cast heavy skins the two boilers looked like huge dormant pachyderms enclosed by a bright fence, truncated featureless monsters, but alive. They never moved, never quivered, made no sound. Yet they seemed to live. Of huge weight, they enclosed within their bellies a tremendous sleeping power, hundreds of compressed degrees of heat, piled up energy bursting to split free.

I do not here remark on the content, e.g. on the fact that Mr Sansom has twice said that the monsters were or seemed alive, and twice that they were sleeping. It is the words to which I draw attention: no one word contains or suggests more than it says. One will not insist, therefore, that every word is 'working', since none is working very intensely; it is a very. English kind of English, quiet, methodical, phlegmatic, unimaginative and admirable for its domestic virtues. The reference to heat brings to my mind an adjective used in a story by Elizabeth Bowen to convey the effect of summer heat on a room: she said that one got the smell of the pitched pine 'exasperated' by heating. The word 'exasperated' is at the opposite pole from this language of conscientious realism.

I began by saying that language in the short-story has, in our time, become much more alert or engrossed, and I set out to illustrate what I mean. I cannot help thinking that the factually meticulous realistic style is a step backward technically (away from this engrossed alertness) though, in my taste, it is a brutal and spiritless and sluggish weapon at all times. Wherever there is wit, or an imaginative stir of humour or passion, or concentration of observation, we will find the more suggestive language leaping across deserts of literalness, and we chase after it to its glittering oasis. Emma Bovary listening to the romantic melancholy of the *Génie du Christianisme* hears it 'se répétant à tous les échos de la terre et l'éternité'; and as she looks at the picture-books, 'en soulevant de son haleine le papier de soie des gravures, qui se levait à demi-plié et retombait doucement contre la page', she saw ladies qui effeuillaient une marguerite de leurs doigts pointus,' and the 'paysages blafards des contrées dithyrambiques' and lakes 'où se détachent en écorchures blanches, sur un fond d'acier gris, des cygnes qui nagent.' And this is the language of the master of Naturalism whose *mots justes* dilate even while they define. For, it does not matter in what school a writer establishes himself, his language must, under challenge, expand its normal voltage by becoming, in the literal sense, more radiant, throwing off new extensions of meaning like an exploding star, if he will but let it—if he has the passion to make it do so. The besotted realists, like Zola, never could do this. Their method always was to pile words on words, detail on detail. Zola never could have used words in such a way as Anatole France did in—'Les cieux, qu'on croyait incorruptibles, ne connaissent d'éternel que

268

l'éternel écoulement des choses'; or 'La voûte solide du firmament est brisée'—two sentences in the first two pages of *Le Jardin d'Epicure* that I chance to open. In the short-story, where the challenge, by virtue of deliberate concentration on a specially selected episode, is always being made, this language, it seems to me, is the chosen weapon.

THE GREAT O'NEILL
Sean O'Faolain

First published in 1942 the intervening years have confirmed *The Great O'Neill's* standing as a modern classic. For nine years O'Neill resisted English expansion in Ulster and in so doing became one of the most famous soldiers in Europe. Though full of drama this book remains a work of immense scholarship.

IRISH POETS IN ENGLISH
Edited by Sean Lucy

This series of Thomas Davis Lectures gives an account of Anglo-Irish poetry from its beginnings to the present day and explores in various ways the different qualities and influences which gave it interest and excellence.

THE ENGLISH LANGUAGE IN IRELAND
Edited by Diarmaid O Muirithe

These nine essays focus on different aspects of the English language in Ireland: its distinctive difference from the English spoken in England or America; the many and varied effects of Ireland's native tongue upon the English language; the Anglo-Irish idiom in works of major Irish writers; dialect and local accent.

www.ingramcontent.com/pod-product-compliance
Lightning Source LLC
Chambersburg PA
CBHW021221090426
42740CB00006B/316